MW01680473

Living Single in a Double World

Living Single in a Double World

by

Marjorie Barton

eShore

Pittsburgh, PA

CeShore

ISBN 1-58501-004-9

Trade Paperback
© Copyright 1999 Marjorie Barton
All rights reserved
First Printing—1999
Library of Congress #98-88776

Request for information should be addressed to:

CeShore Publishing Co.
The Sterling Building
440 Friday Road
Pittsburgh, PA 15209
www.CeShore.com

Cover design: Michelle Vennare - CeShore
Typesetting: Drawing Board Studios
CeShore is an imprint of SterlingHouse Publisher, Inc.

All rights reserved. No part of this publication may be reproduced, stored in a retrieval system, or transmitted in any form or by any means—electronic, mechanical, photocopy, recording or any other, except for brief quotations in printed reviews—without prior permission of the publisher.

Printed in Canada

Contents

Acknowledgements

It is time to thank all those singles who have crossed my paths the last 30 years. If you recognize your story but find the names and places changed; believe, yes, it is probably your story. There is NO fiction in this book.

Thanks to Junette Snyder and many others who said, “Put it in a book.” Thanks again to those who took time to answer my very informal surveys. Again and again they confirmed my thoughts about single life. Thanks to the person in the Waterville, Washington, area who said, “If your column on singles was the only thing in the paper, I would want the paper.” I knew my little messages were needed and read.

Thanks to the young man who worked for a radio station who said, “I wouldn’t miss your column for the world.” He let me know in his way that even young men liked it. Thanks to Grady Auvil, a well-known orchardist in Washington who helped me in many ways, but also liked to discuss what I wrote in my “singles column.” I forever teased him, because he was obviously a happily married man. He said my words were important.

Thanks must go to the high school sweetheart I married, who found me a few years after his first wife died. He came along during the third or fourth rewrite of this book and understood that I have a long list of books to write. He has a special patience I appreciate and he needs in order to live with a formerly long-time single person.

Again, the 26 years of single life taught me that it is not an unpardonable sin to be single and I have an understanding of single life I could never have had if God had not allowed me to be in that position. I thank Him.

Marjorie Barton is my maiden name; I wrote newspaper columns under Marjorie Simmons (married name) and now am married to Edward Wilderman.

Introduction

The first time I wrote comments about living single in a double world was called Page 3 in the newsletter for a singles' group in Port Lavaca, Texas. The first time was on an impulse and everyone wanted me to continue so I did. As I worked for newspapers part time and then became an editor, I developed a column for those living single. It went through various names according to the geographic location until it evolved to LIVING SINGLE IN A DOUBLE WORLD.

As I wrote those columns off and on for about seven years, I was frequently asked to gather the best and put them in book form. It was an intention which finally became a reality. After several edits and revisions, here it is.

Because I had been single for so many years, I began to consider myself somewhat an authority on single parenting, single life and how the rest of the world treated us and expected us to behave. I am not an authority in all matters but I surely have a lot of experience. I clipped and copied articles and statistics about the single population which are quoted or referred to in the book.

The total number of single people has not varied a whole lot in percentages for several years but the categories have shifted somewhat with the never-marrieds gaining considerably. I had read about percentages in various articles over the years but only recently researched to translate the percentages into actual numbers. By this writing the number of singles over 18 in the U.S. has risen to close to 90 million (40 percent) about 26 million (ten percent of the total population) living alone. An astounding forty-four million (23 or 24 percent of adults) are reported to be never-married. Apply those figures to your town or city and you will be amazed.

The purposes of this book are many.

May reading this book give you the courage to remain single if you wish. May it help prepare you to be single if you are not. May it help you find peace in being single if you become single. May it help you have the grace to be single even though you do not prefer that life. May it help you understand single people if you do not. Through it all may it guide you to ideas you never had, help you laugh when it is a good medicine and have faith when you have fear. Most of all may it help you to know it is all right to be single and that you must not let anyone tell you otherwise.

M.B.

NOTE: All anecdotes are true, but names and places have been changed to protect those who have an asterisk by the name.

ONE
LIFE IN THE SINGLE LANE

What is life like in the single lane? Is it more fun? Are there more or different problems? Is it lonely? Is it acceptable? Is there more freedom? Obviously singles have the same emotions that married people have. Singles can save money in the same manner that married people can save money. Singles can go to the same schools, make goals, watch rainbows, plant flowers, go to church and take a walk. So why all the fuss? What makes us think it is different? Because it is! It is time to take a close look at the differences and talk about bridging the gap between singles and marrieds.

The U.S.A. is a place of freedom (so thought the forefathers). The U.S.A. has become a place which fights discrimination (and may be slightly successful). The U.S.A. is a land of many cultures which includes those of different nationalities, colors and language backgrounds. Groups have even been labeled as "cultures" by their geographic location (southern, Appalachia). Is there now another group in the United States referred to but non-labeled as a culture? What shall we call the single population of the United States? Is it a culture? Does it have particular and to some, peculiar characteristics?

Singles have been put down, questioned and even harassed by the married population (often including the church). Singles exist in every race, every geographic location, every city, every village and in rural areas. This book is written to justify, smile upon, admire, and boost the morale and self-esteem of those who are single by choice or fate. It is time to take a close look at singles — their lives, their treatment. This is not the year 1900 but it appears attitude adjustment has not matched the pace of technology when it comes to dealing with singles.

Any person who is never-married, who has lost a spouse by death or who is divorced is the single person discussed here. This writing will not discuss or cover problems of two women, two men, or a man and woman who live "as a couple in a sexual arrangement." Some states recognize living together sexually for a stated time as a "common-law" marriage. Those people are counted in some ways in the census but their numbers do not change the whole drastically so there is no effort to add or subtract them. Many adults live with a parent or a sibling or a child or a non-sexual friend. They are not in the category of "singles living alone" when counted by the census but are single and counted as such.

Life in the single lane has its advantages and disadvantages. Some singles are extremely happy and satisfied. Others admit they are looking for the right mate. Still others find it very difficult to adjust to single life, especially if they have been in a couple relationship very long. Let's take a hard look at some of the good and bad in single life.

Crazy Coupons that don't fit!

Two-for-one coupons abound in the double world, but apparently marketing experts seldom provide many benefits for those living single. One would assume that marketing experts would at some point learn that at least 25 million people live alone in the United States. According to the most recent census another 60 million are single but have a child or housemate. Most single people have less money per capita than do those who are in a double life (as in marriage or co-habitants), but there seem to be less coupons and bargains that fit their lifestyle, according to Tracey Longo in an article for "Kiplinger's Personal Finance Magazine."

It does appear that most fast food coupons are geared to two people. The only thing worse than fast foods are fast foods warmed over, so not very many singles will buy two hamburgers for the price of one or two chicken dinners or any such item. A recent promotional coupon book in an Oklahoma town of 40,000 has more than 20 coupons for specials on pizzas — the second one free or for less money if the first is purchased at the regular price. Those coupons in the book will only work if there is a second person or some one with an enormous appetite or if the single person is having a party.

Grocery stores have long been guilty of catering to the "families" while expecting the millions who live alone to pay a much higher price to obtain a grocery supply. Grocers tend to offer the best prices to those who need to or can buy food by the bulk such as ten or twenty pounds of steak at a time. One option of course, is to buy the steak package big enough to feed a family of twelve twice and divide it into many, many meals if a freezer is available. Nearly all meats in the pre-packaged world of the nineties are much too much for one person. The day of going to a meat counter to choose meat is probably gone forever (There are a few of those).

A recent grocery ad was for fifteen pounds of potatoes for 88 cents. It takes a long time for one person to use fifteen pounds of potatoes, plus it is almost impossible to use them all before they spoil. The alternative is usually to buy five pounds for 99 cents or twenty cents a pound instead of six cents a pound at the sale price. The sad fact is that many of the 25 million who live alone can barely afford the bargain prices.

Perhaps we are too shy. After shopping in one store for a while, I finally had enough courage to ask the produce man if I could buy a smaller amount than the pre-packaged cauliflower and broccoli. He was very nice and cut and wrapped a cauliflower. I have never seen one-half a cauliflower for sale. Broccoli is usually in a bunch with a large rubber band. That grocer said, "Do take part of it, any time."

Fast food outlets are not the only guilty promoters of two for one. An airline recently advertised a "Two for One" trip to Alaska. It would be nice if one person could go two times or one ticket could be discounted 50 percent but that is usually not an option. Most travel specials advertised are all priced for double occupancy, which may discourage the meek and mild from attempting to travel.

Singles Center is a computer "on-line" organization which has a magazine for singles on-line. A report in their "Singles" magazine states that airlines limit the use of frequent flier miles to spouses only. "The International Airline Passengers Association calls this a 'non-issue,' due to the constantly changing whims of singles when it comes to whom they are dating. Many single executives who fly a lot do not agree. Hotels and cruise ships charge double room rates even if one person is occupying the room. Although some tour operators will try to match you with a compatible same-sex roommate—the fact is, a single person is still inconvenienced simply because they do not have a partner.

Some relatively new magazines on the market cater to those over fifty which of course has a large single population. The "Singles" magazine available On-Line at Singles Center and some church affiliated singles' magazines may have more appeal for the young to mid-life singles. As the population of the country ages, more opportunities may appear for single seniors to enjoy the later years.

It may be more than a joke that eating alone, living alone and travelling alone is hazardous to health. Singles should consider joining others in all aspects of life at least part of the time. That is not to say that eating, living and travelling has to be bad or dangerous. Those who always eat alone do not especially prepare the most nutritious meals. Those living alone can tend to neglect some matters of health. Travelling alone requires using simple precautions.

The single never-married female appears to have the longest life expectancy. Although they may be happy and do many things alone, most of them seem to be involved in a lot of activities with others.

Life is a Dance

The message of a popular song in the nineties was that life is like a dance that you learn as it happens. Truth can be found in that statement in that most learning does come from experience. Edith McCall reminds us that most have enough talent and energy to do some very lively dancing mentally if not physically, for many years past middle age. McCall's book *Sometimes We Dance Alone* was published when she was past 80. She had been single for many years, according to the book's introduction.

Ms. McCall insists that alone does not have to mean lonely. She compares life to a ballroom and says that those who choose to sit along the wall are going to miss adventures. I agree with her that if people only sit in front of the TV sitcoms, we should have a mourning party for them (51)!

In *Ageless Body, Timeless Mind* Deepak Chopra said that in order to stay alive a body must be ready for constant change. He explained the physical changes that occur in every body every day, week and year. People who find themselves single after many years of married life need to accept the change but remain as active as possible as Ms. McCall and Dr. Chopra suggested (9).

After the shock of a mate's death or a divorce wears off or the never-married decides it's a life-thing, most soon realize they must prepare to do life's dance alone.

An acceptance of the idea of finishing life's dance alone is a hard choice for some. Others accept gracefully. Some who are single again accept it as a challenge and a regained freedom. Others have no plans to marry. Their plans are to dance alone and for various reasons choose a lifestyle of singlehood.

Placing importance on a successful career has caused many to opt for a single life. Many think that after they enjoy a successful career they might enjoy married life but for many it never happens. The never-married population continues to increase percentage-wise in the U.S. more than any other segment of population (Census On-Line 1998). It appears that more are deliberately planning to do life's dance alone, although many personal interviews would not indicate this. Marriage may be planned for later, but seems to happen less and less.

Many career oriented young singles anticipate a happy marriage somewhere in their future. They often want the career first, marriage second. The association with church and community single groups and casual single friends can help them while they dance alone.

Lonely in the Single Lane

Dr. Perry Treadwell says that loneliness has been defined as being alone when you don't want to be alone. It is natural to feel lonely, but Dr. Treadwell goes further to explore and define how people often substitute for belonging. Dr. Treadwell explains how we overeat, overwork, drink alcohol, seek sex or use drugs, all in an effort to compensate for the need to belong (118-120).

Instead of seeking the company of others, many singles focus on what Dr. Treadwell has labeled an addictive attachment. If understanding the reason for an addictive attachment will help singles, the steps to overcoming the problem may be easier. No doubt many who have an addictive attachment do not realize it is deeply embedded in the need to belong. As the need to belong may be satisfied with attachment to support groups, a thorough discussion of support groups and making friends is in Chapter Four.

Fun in the Single Lane

Many young singles say they prefer life in the single lane because it gives them a freedom that will be gone forever, if or when they marry and have children. To put it in very plain language: they are having fun. They stay out late many nights, maintain a job, perhaps share an apartment, spend their spare time in any hobby such as hunting, fishing, golf, shopping, travelling.

Mid-young singles, whether they had an earlier marriage that ended or not, often insist that they do not mind their life-style. They especially like the freedom to be their own boss, but as more than one who responded to the survey said, "I do want to settle down and have a family, but now I have fun and I'm busy (with my business or job)." Others in the single lane recognize the little unfair acts they encounter but don't seem to put up much of a fight to correct the injustices. They are not rebels.

Perhaps some of the younger generation is having enough fun to overlook society's unfair acts and labels. The next chapter will confront some of those issues that appear as big as mountains to some singles.

TWO
LIFE'S MOUNTAINS

Life in the single lane may be fun for some, but for others it means overcoming one obstacle after another. One of the biggest problems for many may be that of feeling out of place in the couple world. Finances present a problem to many. Others face subtle or not so subtle discrimination. Others face pressures to marry when they are happy single.

Originally my ability to research for information concerning the single population was limited to the library and a wide network of single friends. Add to that computers. Perhaps I should say that most of my suppositions of the past 25 years now seem verified by magazine articles and computer on-line articles.

In order to add to my knowledge and suppositions I decided to survey a few single people. The survey prepared is *casual* and was distributed in a *non-scientific* manner. That does not mean it is invalid. It means none of us can use the information therein as speaking for all singles in the United States. The three surveys were designed with slight differences to be answered by never-married, single by divorce and single by death. Copies of the questions are in the appendix. The surveys were distributed in nine states to church groups, a literary agency, a government agency, a Veteran of Foreign War Post, a nursing agency, a corporate insurance office and a doctor's office. Replies were received from nearly every group. Less than 200 surveys were distributed with about a 25 percent return rate.

In 25 years of being single and being involved in single groups as a leader/publicist/columnist I had ample opportunity to personally interview many people. Many single people were interviewed for news stories which became background information for parts of this book. Many people who fit all the categories of singlehood have crossed my path although I admit I am not as personally knowledgeable of the lifestyle of eastern big city singles. That knowledge is limited so it is impossible for me to be sure I present an accurate picture.

Considering I was an educator, a newspaper publisher and editor and a church leader, my range of acquaintances is wide and varied. I fully believe that 95 percent of my comments on single life fit the greater majority of those who are single by choice or chance.

The Intent to Couple

How many never-married persons have you met who intended to NOT marry from childhood forward? Of course there are some out there. Some do decide at some point in early adulthood that they do not want to marry. When some singles are about 30 they decide the lifestyle of singlehood is acceptable and they are not going to worry about marriage. I have known some never-married mid-life adults who were so shy they would probably never reveal their dreams easily nor would they admit they are afraid to be married.

Usually about the time a 30ish never-married decides he or she is no longer concerned about marriage he is confronted with parents or other relatives who are pushing for just that thing. Forty year-old Richard* settled on the west coast after being in the military service. He likes the climate but every year he enjoys his August visit with his family in upstate New York. He usually helps his dad with special projects around the home. His mother looks forward to his arrival especially because she always has a "nice Catholic girl" picked out for him. He dutifully meets the girl and when his visit is over, returns to his job out west.

Richard is like many singles who have bought a house, had several girl friends, saved money, but never married. He cannot verbalize a reason for not being married, but he is sometimes amused at his mother's efforts.

Fears of Coupling

After difficult relationships that were hard to end and observing the plight of oft-divorced people, the younger generation may have acquired fears and doubts about walking down the aisle of matrimony. Only time will tell if they learned by their observations and if they marry, they are able to marry wisely.

One 30ish single mom of a three year old recently said, "No daddy is better than a drugged daddy," indicating that she would never marry just to acquire a daddy for her daughter. She also agrees that it is more important to acquire skills for bettering life than it is to find a husband. She is concerned with acquiring excellent parenting skills and better job skills. This is scarcely the attitude of the 1930s or 40s or even the 50s.

Another detriment to coupling is the awareness of all types of abuse. Neither male nor female has to put up with a verbally or physically abusive spouse just to go along with attitudes of the double world. Young people seem less apt to tolerate abuse now than in former years. They know it is not acceptable, not necessary and no relationship is worth putting up with it.

Some, again not all of the never-married, say they saw too much dissension, too many divorces and too much unhappiness to feel that marriage is a necessary part of life. Those admissions may be one of the reasons for later marriages or no marriages. The average age for a first marriage is now mid-twenties, meaning that many marriages are taking place much later (Census Information). It will be interesting to look at the statistics twenty years from now to see if the divorce rate lowers because of later marriages.

Who Decided on a Coupled World?

Early biblical teachings did reveal God's plan of only one wife but after Adam and Eve sinned, the situation soon changed. Later on biblical teachings spoke emphatically about marriage and taking care of widows. Biblical laws even had a plan for providing a second husband for a woman whose husband died before old age. In biblical history it appeared marriage was the acceptable standard even if it meant sharing a husband. Somewhere along the avenue of history and with Christian teachings it became preferred in most parts of the world that one man and one woman mate as husband and wife without the continual addition of more wives. Variations on this theme are not the issue here. The concern of this book is the separation of the single world and the double world, not a discussion of marital patterns therein.

Perhaps for the past few centuries parents have purposely taught the desirability of a "family" as in mother, father, children. While the teaching went on, the parents were inadvertently or otherwise espousing the shame of being single. Being single equated with being unloved, unwanted, unhealthy, strange, unstable, ugly, and other undesirable traits.

It is no wonder that so many marriages end in divorce now that divorce has been made so easy. If divorce was difficult to obtain in centuries past, no doubt countless people spent their days miserably married in order to satisfy society's expectations.

The children of the 60s heard about independent living, independent thinking and freedom of choice in profession. Those learning experiences may have resulted in more career-oriented men and women who stay single, but it did nothing for their acceptance in the double world.

Having lived in that single world for a long time I can truthfully say I never met a single who did NOT like the companionship of married people. Being single does not equate with disliking familes. Ask any long time married people how often they purposefully socialize with several singles. If they answer, "rarely," they are merely confirming the remarks of this book. If they were socializing proportionate to the population they would invite three or four singles every time they had a party for twelve. The singles would not be invited in order to match-make. Singles who are past the stage of late night parties usually enjoy family outings and social gatherings very much.

When I lived in the Methow Valley of North Central Washington I had been single 20 years. One family in the valley of many orchards often invited me to stop in and visit. More than once that family invited me to share in a back yard picnic in which most attendees were families. A single man who was employed by the orchardist also attended. We were about the same age and we had some conversation but it was assuredly no attempt to match-make. I told my hosts enthusiastically how I appreciated gathering with other families. They did not think it was strange as it was their nature to do such things. It had not been a common occurrence in my single life. Will we ever overcome this false illusion that singles and married people cannot socialize?

Discrimination?

While I lived in that area of Washington state I substituted for four school districts so only the guilty can relate to this story. At one of the schools I was visiting with another substitute teacher named Jan*. She said that she had moved there in order to be near the mountains for skiing and other outdoor activities. We discussed the possibility of full-time teaching positions.

"I don't know why I stay here," Jan confided. "In the six years I've been here they've never hired an unmarried person. I have checked it out. It's been true for a long time, even before I came. I know I'm wasting my time. I need to go to another area while I can, so I can have leave time and insurance benefits."

"Oh, dear," I replied. "I'm doubly cursed, single and past being young. I just thought my age was the detriment."

It was true that there was a general surplus of teachers at that time, but not a surplus in special education, an area in which I could claim a lot of experience. Although I substituted in that school again I did not see Jan. Discrimination based on sex or marital status is not ever easy to prove. However, it is easy in a relatively small school district for the board members to have quiet, unwritten agreements about sexual preference or marital status. This incident DID occur when discrimination laws were in place. I managed to stay in that area (also my geographical preference). I gave up the idea of a teacher's contract and found a job in the insurance industry.

Before I moved to Washington I spent several years teaching in Texas where I experienced discrimination of another kind. After a year in one community I was able to purchase a very dilapidated old house (on a private contract). My credit union had a new policy concerning unsecured loans which enabled me to borrow $2500 for repair. That took care of everything but the roof. Children and friends helped me remove wallpaper, dirt, and even walls to redo the old house. New paint, clean walls and new floor covering made it quite attractive and livable, but the roof was in constant need of patching.

As I had used the same bank for four years I approached the loan officer for money to replace the roof. (The credit union had changed its rules again so no more funds were available there). I was turned down for the loan which the banker casually declared was based on my income.(It was never in writing). A couple of years later I sold the house to someone whose income appeared to be lower than mine. The person who bought the house was able to finance the total price of the house plus money for repairs.

One might assume it was a gender thing and not a single thing except for one bit of evidence. I knew the loan officer so I asked how this man managed such a big loan using the same collateral I had been turned down for?

The bank officer explained, "Well, he's a family man and the bank likes that."

I was appalled as I knew the man's job as a laborer at a construction company probably paid less than my teacher's salary.

In the late 1990s other areas of discrimination still exist, according to articles in a singles' magazine available via computer on-line. Taxes, insurance, housing/rent laws as well as health and travel were issues addressed in the fall of 1997. Via computer internet "*The Singles Center*" said it presented the series of articles aimed to "illuminate a few choice injustices done to single people."

In addition to the on-line articles is an example in the tax structure in the state of Kansas. *The Kansas City Star* (MO) headline was "High Court Rebuffs Challenge to Kansan's Tax Rates for Singles." The news story said that without comment the justices left intact a Kansas court ruling that called the uneven tax system a legitimate way to encourage people to get married. Since 1988 married couples filing joint returns have paid lower rates than single people at the same income level in Kansas (May 20, 1997).

According to another article, although insurance rates may no longer be based on gender, being married at certain ages lowers the rate in some states. Is the supposition that marriage makes one a better driver? It is understandable to have the rates higher for the young drivers if the accident rate continues to be higher. Saying a married 18 year old is a better driver than a single 18 year old would probably be very difficult to prove.

How does the double world determine all these strange assumptions are true? The same assumptions prevail concerning housing and rental laws. In a very recent time one of my daughters informed me that I should pretend she was married if I ever met her landlady! The rules of the complex were that a person should be married, not merely have a housemate. I asked others in the area and was assured that was not a fictitious situation. They had confronted the issue more than once. The Single Center's stories on housing discrimination commented that with more than 86 million single adults, the single population certainly consists of more than unruly twenty-somethings (1998).

More Mountains to Climb

Some young people may aspire to climb mountains or to win Olympic medals, but few expect to have to climb mountains of discrimination and misconcepts if they remain single. When parents are raising children to adulthood they tend to hope for what they believe is an ideal life for each child. They hope for a well-adjusted adult who will acquire an education appropriate to his abilities and who will settle into a family situation providing them with fine grandchildren. I never meet a parent who doesn't wish the best for his or her children, at least what the parent thinks is the best. Parents with handicapped children are aware of many problems that may emerge but few parents anticipate dealing with issues of homosexuality or children who never marry.

Many a never-married adult or one who is single for any reason has to deal with their own parents' attitudes toward them in addition to society's pressures to fit into a mold. A few singles are fortunate to have understanding parents or parents who accept decisions they make as adults. Other singles have to encounter the "When are you going to find the right girl (or boy) and settle down?" question every time they go to a family gathering. After the family members tire of that question they may ask "Are you still single?"

Terms that fit families such as "ideal" or "perfect" never seem to be applied to a single. Have you ever heard that he or she is a perfect single or an ideal single? Dr. Janice Witzel teaches at the Family Institute of Northwestern University in Evanston, Illinois, as I write this book. She says that staying single is often considered a personal failing (Toufexis 52-55).

According to Dr. Witzel, never-married women are often described as having deficiencies. On the other hand men, according to writer Ron Beathard, are criticized as being impractical, maintaining a fantasy of perfection and of avoiding family and parental involvement. In a column for "Newsweek" Mr. Beathard says that men have been accused of being too self-centered to have children and that they avoid commitment. He does not accept the criticisms he receives (12).

Dr. Witzel set out to disprove some theories about never-married women by writing a dissertation on the subject. Her study found that the respondents were happy, satisfied with life work, and well-adjusted (53).

In an article in Psychology Today Anastasia Toufexis says that no common pattern emerges among the never-married. She says they come from all socio-economic groups. The never-married are as likely to have had nurturing, supportive parents as abusive, destructive ones and to have had positive examples as well as negative ones (52-55).

Studies about never-married women indicate that most had the same basic wants: a career, a husband, and a family. Mr. Beathard laughingly points out that no one studies never-married men but a recent census report indicates there are more never-married men than women. (Surprise?)

The "I don't fit" Syndrome

Married people having single friends does not equate with married people socializing with singles. Ask us. Married people are not unfriendly to singles, just rarely sociable.

The informal surveys I described continue to arrive in the mail. Another person just made the comment "I didn't fit" which has been made voluntarily by numerous people, both on the surveys and in interviews over the years. The comments are usually from people returning to the single world after a marriage (of any length).

It does not seem an intention of couples to be unfriendly toward singles. It is that they just don't seem to consider inviting them to private social events. The most recent survey received had the comment, "I had to make new friends immediately (after divorce)."

A never-married friend who did live in the Washington, D. C. area, says that she had a married friend she often lunched with but that she never met the woman's husband. My friend's work and her volunteer activities put her in touch with a lot of marrieds and singles. She has seen a few long time friends go through marriage and divorce, but readily admits that true social events have been with singles.

The best way to solve the "I don't fit" syndrome is to search for new friends. The very daring might confront some of the old married friends with straightforward questions, but it likely will depend on each individual circumstance as to the content of the answer.

As singles climb what they consider to be mountains of problems, they may solve them if they watch out for the sign posts as discussed in the next chapter.

THREE
LIFE'S SIGNPOSTS

My Philosophy of Signposts

No doubt there would be less calamities on the highways if Americans obeyed the signposts. All the subheadings in this chapter have appeared on highway signposts in the United States. The multitude and variety of signposts has fascinated me for many years. At one time a few years ago I used the words from highway signposts as headings for one-liners in my weekly newspaper column. This chapter is an attempt to use the words from highway signposts as metaphorical suggestions as to what may happen in single life.

Watch for Falling Rocks

Life is often difficult and has unexpected events. You may think a boulder landed in the middle of your road of life if you just experienced an unexpected death or divorce. Even an *expected* death or divorce may cause you to think rocks are falling on you.

More than one writer and/or psychologist has given labels to the time frame after losing a spouse by death. Denial, anger, despair, bargaining and acceptance seem to cover any terms used by various people. The stages apply to all forms of loss including a spouse by divorce. (The terms may not be applicable if the remaining spouse considers the divorce a riddance rather than loss.)

Dr. Jane Hannah is an assistant professor in the Department of Pediatrics at Vanderbilt University and is a single mother. In a Question and Answer section of "Christian Single" magazine she described sudden grief similar to having an amputation without anesthesia (24).

If impact and denial are used to describe the first weeks or months following when a person becomes single again, specific words used to characterize that state of mind are: numbness, shock, disbelief. During that initial time of bereavement and/or divorce action, friends and relatives often make attempts to be supportive and helpful. By the time reality sets in those same friends and relatives may wrongly assume the victim has sufficiently recovered to be on his or her own without further assistance.

Actually, it is when reality sets in that most single-again people need some support and guidance even more than at first. As the victim comes out of shock, friends and relatives go on about their daily lives, not necessarily meaning to be neglectful, but perhaps not realizing the needs of the bereaved or divorced. Those who have had the experience are usually the only ones able to help anyone else through it. (About support groups, next chapter)

While financial problems, children's needs, and loneliness raise their cantankerous voices, the bereaved, divorced and bewildered attempt to move on in life. As they engage in work or activities and meet old friends, they are nearly always faced with a decision about how to answer the usual question, "How are you today?" Is it appropriate to tell the truth about feelings or should people pretend everything is fine? Perhaps a little honesty would help friends and relatives know that help and encouragement are still needed. Regardless of the reasons, not everyone lets others know his or her true feelings.

When W. Clement Stone, founder of Combined Insurance Company of America, developed his sales training courses, he insisted on one thing. Salesmen must act enthusiastic and smile, whether they felt like it or not. Stone taught and claimed that if a person pretended to be enthusiastic, he would soon forget that it was a pretense and actually become enthusiastic. The same with a smile, Stone believed that if a person acted happy and smiled, he most probably could and would be happy (Hill and Stone, 141-142).

As iceskater Ekaterina Gordeeva told her mother, there didn't seem to be any purpose in her life after her young husband died of a heart attack. Her mother reminded her of her daughter, Daria. Ekaterina's mother told her Daria did not need a sick mom and that she should try to be a healthy person again. She found healing in her work, which is often the tonic for countless bereaved people. Time is a healer and work helps pass the time (77).

Water on Roadway

It is not appropriate to drive through deep water on a road, but when calamities occur in life it may take a lot of tears on life's roadway before recovery takes place. When loss is present in life, it is all right to cry. Books have been written about recovering from loss: loss of spouse, loss of job, loss of pet, loss of best friend, loss of children, loss of property. A loss is a loss. Being sad is part of the process of recovery. Everyone has a right to cry and no one should feel ashamed or embarrassed.

In *How to Heal Depression* authors Harold H. Bloomfield, M.D. and Peter McWilliams remind us that it is possible to have a healthy sadness. A healthy sadness is free from self-pity and suffering that goes with depression. The authors also said that feeling bad is not a bad feeling (146).

Thirty-year-old Steve* is a carpenter in a small town in Missouri, where he grew up. He doesn't want to move away, but he is sad to be alone.

He has recently ended a year long relationship and is quite perplexed by his own reaction of being so sad. Steve goes to a restaurant/bar "because I can't cook", eats his evening meal and laughs and visits with friends. When he arrives home each evening, the tears flow. "I'm so sad," he says, "and I just don't know what to do." At last report Steve was doing better because he realized it is acceptable to be sad for a while after a loss.

Most attempt to shed tears in privacy, which is less embarrassing and can be healing. If healing is taking place, the tears should begin to subside more quickly after their onset and should not be an everyday occurrence.

While everybody cries from time to time, few people understand the biological reasons for crying. It can be brought on by anger, pain and happiness as well as sadness. A feeling of stress and despair can certainly bring on tears. Crying can also be a cleansing. As water cleanses the body, so tears may cleanse the mind and soul. After a "good cry", one's mind and soul may seem fresh and new and able to go on to face the next day with a smile instead of a frown.

A community singles' club in South Texas had many planned activities, including a specified time each month for discussing specific topics. One month the topic was depression. The discussion leader explained about the various kinds of depression, suggested reading material, and explained about crying.

One of the group was a guide fisherman named Hank*, known state-wide for his expertise. He was very large in stature. The group of single friends called him "the big fisherman." He was assumed to be tough.

In the discussion Hank said he was so glad to learn that others cried because he thought there was something wrong with him. He explained that he sometimes felt like crying, although he didn't know why, but he cried until he felt better.

The most important discovery by some is to understand that crying is not limited to women or old people. It is all right to cry. A reasonable amount of crying is usually appropriate and beneficial. It may not be totally understood, but crying can relieve tension and help put aside grief, perhaps better than medication.

No Services for 81 Miles

Perhaps it depends on attitude if you assume a long stretch of highway will be boring. If the road of your life seems boring, tiresome, and downright wearying, it is probably time for a life-analysis. Boredom is often a disguised form of depression. If life seems to have lost its reasons for continuing, it may be perceived as boring. Depression may interfere with the mind's ability to program itself to do things that need to be done. You may require the services of a professional to determine whether your problem is boredom or depression.

Depression is often situational and temporary. It can usually be overcome without seeing a doctor. Change of activity and deliberate exercise often help overcome mild depression. It is very important to know the difference between clinical depression or justified sadness (temporary depression). If you have just experienced a loss, you are probably experiencing temporary depression as part of your grief recovery process.

Bloomfield and McWilliams and others are quick to point out that depression is the probably the number one public health problem in the country. These authors state that one in twenty Americans suffer from depression severe enough to require medical treatment and that one in five will have a depression at some time in life (4).

Insomnia, fatigue, anxiety, stress, vague aches and pains, and a desire to sleep excessively are common symptoms of depression. If you think you need help, don't hesitate. Call your doctor.

When a person is certain a depression is circumstantial and not clinical, there are many ways to overcome temporary feelings of sadness. If sadness has lasted more than a few months and does not seem to lessen, then you should seek a doctor's advice.

Og Mandino is the author of *The Greatest Salesman in the World*. In the story, Mandino presents lessons for living in the form of simple messages on ten scrolls (26).

One of the scrolls suggests that we should be master of our emotions. Mandino explains that all nature is a circle of moods, constantly changing. He says the human is part of nature which also has constantly changing moods. Mandino explains how to master emotions so that every day is a happy day. We need to force our actions to control our thoughts, instead of allowing thoughts to control our actions (26). It would be nice if we could all heed his advice.

Mandino's suggestions are similar to W. Clement Stone's admonition that if you pretend to be enthusiastic, you will become enthusiastic.

Some suggestions are to sing if you feel depressed and to laugh if you feel sad (91). If Stone and Mandino's guidelines seem too idealistic or difficult, they may at least be worth a try. We should recognize that it is not humanly possible to remain in the same constant mood, just as nature is never the same. That understanding should be of some help in coping with problems of sadness and depression.

If boredom or depression are creating problems on your life's road, new activities may eliminate either. Singles can make a list of activities they always intended or wanted to do but didn't have time. Many self-help books recommend the same approach: get out and do something. Even without support groups, singles can pursue new hobbies or revive old ones. Involvement in a hobby — be it hiking, biking, ceramics, community theatre or rock-hunting is a likely way to make new friends and stamp out boredom.

If boredom can be defined as something monotonous, then life filled with boredom becomes like food without salt and spices. The adage that variety is the spice of life needs to be applied.

Singles can search for additional activities rather than searching for the right partner. Friends and partners can often be found within the activities. Local newspapers usually have a schedule of the activities available to the general public. Hospitals and schools can always use volunteers; nursing homes welcome visitors.

Primitive Road - No Warning Signs

Some signs on the real road as well as the road of life really tickle our funny bones. The sign PRIMITIVE ROAD - NO WARNING SIGNS in the mountainous areas of Washington state will make most people laugh because usually in plain view IS a WARNING sign that reads WATCH OUT FOR SNOW PLOWS. Another road sign that caused me to laugh was FARM CROSSING. I did a double-take and thought hard before I figured out that the highway department was trying to tell drivers that the farm was on both sides of the roadway.

Another one that amused me the first time I saw it was GAME BIRDS IN ROADWAY. Having seen hundreds of DEER signs, a few warnings of COWS, a few warnings of ELKS, and falsely believing that birds flew out of the way, I was surprised to see the GAME BIRDS IN ROADWAY sign. The cutest sign I ever saw was on a remote road I had to travel to locate an insurance client. The sign was home-made and it read: OLD MAN CROSSING.

Laughter is important for healing hearts, minds and bodies. The Bible, radio commentator Paul Harvey, author/editor Norman Cousins, and articles in "Psychology Today" all recommend laughter. Proverbs 17:22 states "A merry heart doeth good like a medicine." Paul Harvey has reminded his listeners of his radio commentary that laughter as a medicine has been ordered by doctors for hundreds of years.

In 1979 Norman Cousins claimed that laughter promotes good health in his book *An Anatomy of an Illness.* A 1996 article in "Psychology Today" explained in detail what happens physiologically and psychologically when a person laughs. Dr. John Morreall, president of HUMORWORKS Seminars says that after you laugh you go into a relaxed state, your blood pressure and heart rate drop below normal so you feel profoundly relaxed. He says that laughter also indirectly stimulates endorphins, the brain's natural painkillers (34).

Dr. Morreall says that psychological effects are less obvious. He and Dr. William Fry (same article) both agree that creativity and humor are similar because they both involve bringing together two items which do not have an obvious connection and then creating a relationship. They say that humor also helps us contend with the unthinkable — our mortality (34).

If everyone needs to laugh, you may be thinking what does this have to do with single people? Although the statistics keep reminding us that millions of people have always been single (44 million, remember?), those who become single again often experience a very sad time. They sometimes think they have forgotten how to laugh, that nothing is fun or funny in their new single status. Perhaps they need to learn to laugh again.

People appear to benefit more when they control the type of humor to which they are exposed. "*Psychology Today*" cites a study on patients recovering from surgery at a Florida hospital. The patients who were allowed to choose the humorous movies they saw required fewer painkillers than a control group that saw no movies. A third set of patients watched humorous movies they did not choose and they did the worst of all the patients (37).

Laughter, not tempered with conscientiousness, is not helpful. In other words, laughing while eating unhealthy foods and smoking cigarettes does not extend life nor make you healthier. Laughter accompanied with the excessive use of alcohol has short-lived benefits.

Advice for singles attempting to adjust to a new life is to deliberately add a little humor to life. Rent or go to a humorous movie. Read the humorous story sections in a lot of *Reader's Digests* (new or old).

My long tenure as a single parent included work as a therapy and humor a necessity. I learned early in single life that laughter is the best medicine. I have worn glasses since the age of two and am blind without them. I have often evoked a laugh or two by improper dressing. Because I dress before I put my glasses on, my clothes may be on backwards or wrong side out.

My youngest daughter has been known to stop a catastrophe many times by saying, "Mother, are you going out like that?"

Freshly laundered T-shirts and sweaters are the most

probable problems! I worried a little about how I would get along when that daughter was away from home. Usually, I have caught those mistakes before going out the door. However I recently got out of my car at a Walmart and noticed my jacket sweater was on wrong-side-out just in time to reverse it!

Og Mandino recommends laughter in his lessons for becoming the greatest salesman in the world. Mr. Mandino says that because humans have the ability to laugh they should cultivate the habit of laughter (27).

Wear laughter like a coat, use it appropriately. Apply laughter if possible, when confronting the aspects of life for which there were no warning signs.

Watch out for Blowing Snow (or Sand, or Smoke)

Snow can be very deceitful. So can humans. The soft, silent, deceptive, white flakes act as an insulative blanket for the wheat farmers, help protect fruit trees from winter freeze, but all the while that snow may be setting the stage for a historical flood at melting time. Beautiful snow makes awesome pictures but causes people to lose control of autos or to break a leg. Human deception often appears as well disguised as the winter snow. Those who are newly single again need to be wary of something or someone who appears too good to be true.

Those re-entering single life need to be aware of some of the hazards and pitfalls. Con artists show up in ample numbers to prey on the naive in matters of money as well as romance.

Large single groups in cities usually have strict rules about participants being single, but it is up to each individual to verify marital status before dating. It might save a lot of heartache later. "I am getting a divorce," is not synonymous with "I am divorced."

It is as possible to meet a deceitful person in church as in a bar, though that is sad but true. Kathleen* met her new boyfriend at church. He had a good job and she felt he didn't need her money, although she made the mistake of confiding in him how much she attained in her divorce settlement. It was a substantial amount as a business was involved in the divorce settlement.

Kathleen married her new love. She sadly reported that it took less than two years for him to go through her money. She lamented to me that it was hard to believe the deceit he was able to make her believe. He took his ex-wife and ex-step daughter on a cruise "right under her nose," Kathleen said. Don't shake your head in disbelief. This is a true story.

Incidents such as this cause most people with substantial savings or property to draw up pre-nuptial agreements before marriage. If there are no deceitful plans in the background, neither party should be offended.

"Be ye not deceived by appearances," thus saith this author!

WHERE IS THE SIGN?

According to answers on many of the surveys and my interviews with single people over a 25 year period a very common thread exists. It is like the absence of a road sign when you wish you could see one to direct you. Never-marrieds and single-again people have stated that they are usually not included in activities with married couples. You can argue that point if you happen to be married and have many single social friends, or you can do as I have and ask everyone you know who is single. What happens to friends when a divorce or death occurs? Also ask never-marrieds how many couple friends they have.

Many of the single-again said they felt abandoned by friends and no longer socialized with couples. The never-married seems to have figured some time ago that their friends are usually unmarried. Most of them don't even try to socialize with couples, although many would like to because of their common interests in life. These statements are not all-inclusive because there are always exceptions.

Two of the most recent examples come from a physician and a musician. Both are never-married, under 40, personable, and are interested in socializing with people of similar interests. Both said they had invited couples to do things and been rejected. The woman physician said, "It looks strange and their wives aren't thrilled."

In her book, *Alone and Surviving*, Rae Lindsay said that she feels most married friends drop you because they don't know what to do with you (107).

The dilemma seems to apply to both. Single people don't often know how to socialize with their friends who marry. Perhaps the hope in maintaining or cultivating friendships among the married and unmarried lies in the mutual interests the people might share. Pure socializing should not be the only reason for having friends. Socializing should be a time of companionship developed because of mutual interests when people have a good time being together.

Probably the single-again who suffers the most after death or divorce of a spouse is one whose social life included the same couples again and again. Couples whose activities are highly varied and who have friends in church as well as other social settings may not have such bad experiences when one of them returns to single life.

There is not much argument about the fact that few people are well prepared to re-enter single life after a marriage of 20 years or longer. No doubt those people will be unhappily looking for some sign to guide them to the right path.

BUMP

If you have a bump or a sore that won't go away, do not be a martyr because you are single. Go to a doctor at once.

DETOUR

Expect many detours in single life. Be careful. The road is not always smooth on detours.

SOFT SHOULDERS

Soft romantic shoulders may be inviting. Don't be too tempted; check out the person's attitudes and beliefs. Make sure the attraction is more than soft shoulders.

STOP

Stop! Don't go racing through life without stopping. Check what is coming from all directions. You may be able to avoid a terrible calamity.

Now that you are aware of some of the possible signposts you may confront as a single person, consider the advice of both the professionals and those who have been there and done that. In the next chapter learn more about support groups in the single lane.

FOUR
LIFE'S LEANING POSTS

In *The Pursuit of Happiness* Dr. David Myers talks about individualism. He said that President Ronald Reagan called the late 20th century the age of the individual.

The bereaved, divorced and very independent career singles need to forget the attitude of "individualism" and allow themselves to be a little *DEPENDENT.* Being an individualist may bring about independence but Myers states that numerous studies conclude that people are happier when supported by friends and families (145-148). There are times in every single's life in which friends and groups are needed for support.

People To Lean On

Let's face it, we all need someone to lean on at some point in life. Other times in life will probably find someone leaning on us. Have you ever heard anyone say, "He's a people person."? Surely some people do seem to enjoy and thrive on being around other people nearly all the time. Others seem satisfied with little or no conversation except with those family members or friends they have slowly come to rely on through the years. On close analysis everyone, whether a people person or a more quiet subdued person, wants someone to talk to part of the time.

Ask anyone who has been single or is single — what is the greatest need when living alone? The answer is nearly always the same, "finding someone to talk to."

It is reported in *Science magazine* by Sumiko Oshima (43-44) that Japanese people have the longest life expectancy. One reason is claimed that they have stronger family ties. They do not usually live alone; they have someone with whom to talk. Perhaps it is partly genetic, partly diet, but all research does seem to confirm that the will to live also corresponds to a sense of being needed. If you have no one with whom to talk, you probably do not feel needed. Eventually the lack of feeling needed may cause a decline in the will to live.

Perhaps Americans can lengthen their lives by strengthening ties to their own families or to substitute families. In *The New American Family*, Jerry Falwell claims that many American families have adopted a philosophy that they can make it on their own without attachment to extended family members (40-41). Falwell points out that usually when they suddenly face a major crisis, they find they do need each other.

In *Making Friends, Leaving Loneliness Behind*, Dr. Perry Treadwell describes loneliness as a positive emotion that tells us we need human attachment (32). Formal studies cited by Dr. Treadwell indicate that about 40 percent of single adults consider loneliness to be the greatest disadvantage to being single.

If you question the existence of a loneliness industry, consider these available services. The industry supports singles' magazines and mail and video dating services. Parents Without Partners is nation-wide and supports its own magazine.

A Singles Center is available on the internet, which has a magazine and other services such as a chat room, travel services and special events, a listing of single groups, forums and personals. This is a relatively new business which may be one answer to a vast population of singles who live in sparsely populated areas or in small towns with no obvious activities for singles. As the availability of computer on-line services expands it will afford an opportunity for another segment of single population to stay in touch with other singles.

The Singles Center advocates many worthwhile and admirable activities, such as a foundation to establish scholarships and fund-raisers which will benefit singles or a whole community. Volunteering in communities is part of the Singles Center's promotion. The e-mail address is singlescenter.com. There are many subheadings from which to choose. The Singles Center is available by paid membership and appears to have many supportive ideas for singles nationwide.

RV groups such as LOWS(Loners on Wheels) obviously caters to those who are alone and like to travel and has planned rallies and special events. Dr. Perry Treadwell conducts friendship workshops, which could not be successful or needed if no one was lonely (32). Books are written on how to find new partners, how to cope with death and divorce, and how to be a good single parent. The industry would not be as broad and successful if there were not lots of lonely people. What is this except a loneliness industry? It caters to people who neither want nor need to be alone all the time.

Most who have lost a spouse by death or divorce reach a stage in recovery in which they find or want new friends. Sometimes they find them through a support group. Needing a support group or new friends is not a sign of weakness.

The world is a busy place, but everyone likes to share dreams, sorrows, frustrations and successes with other human beings. This points to a big demand for new systems of emotional support for people who love the independence of solo living yet thirst for companionship and friendship in good times and bad.

Many more community singles groups and church single groups exist than did 20 or 30 years ago. Many mid-sized to large towns have a Parent-Without-Partner chapter or something comparable. Utmost in the minds of many attendees is the goal of new friends with similar situations. The advantages of organized singles should be obvious, but there are still those who insist "they don't need it." Usually the reason for that statement is because of the comments the singles have heard from the double world about searching for a new mate. Neither this book nor countless others advocate living alone, but because it is occurring in greater numbers than in the past, there are more people looking for social outlets to bring a balance to their lives.

Krystal and Dana spent most of their lives in my single parent home and now they are single moms (Is it catching?). They have nothing but praise for PWP groups because of the on-going family activities and friendships established. Children, as well as adults, need to know they are not alone in a new kind of world. Someone should form a support group for children of single parents; perhaps one exists.

In "*Help Yourself Through the Hard Times*" author Collin Perry agrees as he advocates joining a support group. As Perry emphasizes, once you make the decision to 'get on with life,' you'll need someone to talk to—and the most effective kind of conversation can be with someone else who has undergone a similar ordeal (125).

The United States has 65 million people living in rural areas (or towns with less than 2500), in which support groups may not be readily available. It is interesting to note that in the late 1990s that in 36 of the 50 states 35 percent of the people live in rural areas(U.S.Census).

Singles in such small towns and rural areas have a difficult time connecting with other singles. It is possible but much more difficult. One of the big problems is that the smaller the community, the less aware singles are of other singles. Newly divorced or widowed may have to initiate their own plan.

Any single can start a support group by making a list of everyone they know who is a widow, widower, divorced or never married. Mail a post card and/or put up "fliers" around town to meet at some pre-arranged coffee shop or community meeting room. That is what happened in a town in which I taught school. A never-married Methodist pastor arranged to use a bank hospitality room, put up fliers and about 30 people showed up. Out of that group grew a very active singles group. That town's population was about 12,000.

Another town in which I attended college had a singles group which I was told started by a similar method. Members of the community in which I first labeled the column

"Living Single in a Double World" begged me to start a group. The town had only 900 people. I was very reluctant because a leader does a lot of work. I finally gave in and we had a lot of fun though we never attracted the younger singles. I know for a fact there were plenty of younger singles in the community, but no one led out to start a group at that time. Every type of support group ever formed had to have a leader. The organizer does not have to be the leader forever, but it takes time and initiative to form any type of support group.

Yes, I have helped start a group in more than one location. My firm belief is that it can be done in any community. Just think, every town of 40,000 has 28 to 40 percent of its total population living single (and about ten percent of the nation's total population live alone). That translates to about 11,000 single adults in a town of 40,000. I know you are about to disbelieve, but these are 1999 census figures.

Many churches, some banks (hospitality room), and YWCAs or YMCAs are all possible meeting places for organizing various support groups and possibly for continued meetings. Most church single groups are very social. If smaller communities could understand the widespread needs of singles, perhaps they would be more supportive, especially if they realize how many are single. If you are reading these facts for the first time and you live in a rural area or a very small community, you might write a letter to your local newspaper and share some facts about single population figures. Others seeing it in print may realize there are more singles than they imagined.

Some are Silver, Some are Gold - Friends

All friends are valuable. Some friendships from the Double World will fade for various reasons. Friendships are a part of life that are apt to change, but friends are important in the realm of support at times of crises.

Susan Davis wrote an article for *American Health* and said it is a hard pill to swallow when a friendship ends after

12 years. The loss of former close friends after a divorce or death is something unexpected. We must all remember that friendships are voluntary. Job changes, moves, new interests, death, divorce and other factors contribute to changes in friendships. Friendships are affected by change the same as other aspects of life, though some weather every imaginable change (59-62).

Dr. Diane Prusank is a specialist in interpersonal communications who says that our culture is obsessed with romance and has made friendship secondary. Davis and Prusank consider friendships more important than acknowledged by most in recent decades (60). It is true that we want and need all kinds of friends, from the kind who will water our lawn while we are away, to the one we can call in the middle of the night in a crisis.

Friendships need a lot of give and take, just like marriage. Friction can occur when one friend wants more, gives more or even reveals more than the other. Keeping up with friends in the hectic pace of this modern world is not easy, but it is possible. As with any relationship, sometimes we just have to let go when situations or interests change.

Efforts to make new friends are usually rewarding and certainly timely after experiencing the loss of a mate. Friends may be the only support needed at first. Perry Treadwell's book has many ideas for making new friends (225). Some of his ideas include: wear an unusual T-shirt or carry a conversation starter such as a book or pamphlet. Carry a card with your name and number, not necessarily an address, to give to people who interest you. Be open to contact; don't hide behind books or newspapers. Renew old acquaintances; decide which casual friends you would like to know better. Relax. Check newspapers for calendars with events for everyone and choose those you can attend alone. Walk a pet, go window shopping, check out bookstores, libraries, trade shows. Have a nonsignificant party. Invite acquaintances to bring a friend but not their partner (225).

Another opportunity for making friends is through continuing education, either in public schools or local community colleges. Course listings from creative writing to amateur geology (rock-hounding) can be found. Seminars or short courses in investment, cooking, gardening are available sometimes. Another source of short-term school are computer stores. They often conduct or arrange for seminars or a day class to learn a specific software. Many local stores offer classes for crafts or quilting. Collin Perry recommended learning a new skill, which almost assuredly will also bring about new friendships (126). Your local daily paper probably lists many such sources.

Some libraries have sessions for would-be genealogists. Special interest clubs abound: archery, square dancing for singles, photographers, writers, rock-hounds, boaters, skiers, bikers. There are also political clubs. The act of volunteering can be a source of some new friendships and the list of volunteer opportunities is endless.

When life's circumstances change, adults are sometimes out of practice in gaining new friends, but most adults react positively to gestures of friendliness. As the world changes so do friends. Make a friend; be a friend.

Friends are like coats—several are needed. Everyone needs a few casual friends, like a light wind-breaker. These friends easily relate to each other concerning children, school, community, church, or politics, and may be involved in the same activities.

Another friend might be like a dress jacket or coat. These friends can share intellectual interests in books, movies or music. They are also together in church work or perhaps, PTA, but not on a very personal basis.

Friends who are like warm winter coats have usually known each other quite a while. They share both good news and bad and have good feelings after a visit. They intend to keep in touch forever.

Some friends are like a unique western jacket or a blazer that indicates membership in a special organization. That friend always makes a statement. It is positive, encouraging or enlightening. Those friends are not "best" friends but "good" friends. They are optimistic and radiate good attitude.

Hopefully, everyone can have a friend who is like the dependable old jacket that goes camping or to the beach or the mountains...and will never be thrown away. He or she is the friend to rely on in times of trouble, heartbreak, and good news! That is the friend no one wants to be without.

Mr. Treadwell emphasizes that making friends takes time and energy. We must be willing to risk self-exposure, to accept ourselves as well as others. Making friends will require thoughtfulness and the courage to express our feelings (225).

Friends of all types are helpful but it is important in life to establish a strong friendship or two with people who can offer support in times of crises, which are inevitable in the course of living. Singles really need friends.

Latch On To An Optimist

No one needs negative friends, certainly not at a time of new circumstances in life. In the matter of making and keeping friends, new or old, having optimistic ones is almost a necessity. Although an optimistic person might find himself in need of a boost, he also has great coping skills when life's unexpected does occur.

A couple of thousand years ago a teacher named Jesus of Nazareth told his followers to "have faith and nothing shall be impossible to you." (Matthew 17:20) Motivational seminars and pep rallies are being held still expounding that philosophy. Nothing has really changed except the technology used in the attempt to teach optimism or the power of positive thinking. The power of positive thinking is just a new phrase for biblical teachings.

Singles in a double world are interested in succeeding in personal relationships as well as the business world. If singles are in a time of transition, they especially need optimistic friends, even if they have to make extra effort to have them. In *The Pursuit of Happiness*, author David G. Myers, Ph.D. wrote about optimism. He said that happy, optimistic people are filled with hope and that they are healthier. Myers does remind that even optimists must be realistic(27-28).

Dr. Myers suggests a recipe for well-being which requires neither positive nor negative thinking alone. The recipe also has a mix of ample optimism to provide hope, a dash of pessimism to prevent complacency, and enough realism to discriminate those things we can control from those we cannot (119).

In order to have the balance needed in life it appears you need an optimistic friend or two, especially if you are not so optimistic yourself. Set about to make the friendships you need so they will already be established when you are in need. Friends and special support groups are good and necessary but everyone should recognize that life has a spiritual side and develop that part of life, probably by attending the church of your choice, which may be the best support group of all.

The Church Door Is Open

There may not be a church on every corner but there are a lot of churches. (Dr. Myers says there are 300,000 churches). If you have been out of church or never in church, perhaps now is the time to consider a change in that part of your life. Why wait until a crisis such as devastating illness or death enters your life to call upon a church? Church can be the support system for your spiritual life. It is free in the sense of you aren't charged a fee; contributions are voluntary.

Although Christian, Jewish, and most other churches have been highly oriented to promotion of families, a new era of recognition and acceptance for all singles may be at hand. It is impossible to speak for all churches but casual observation of news releases and activities in local churches seem to indicate that more and more support is being offered to the single population. The main truth is that the church won't often reach out and pull you in. You and perhaps a friend may have to make the effort to go together a few times.

Singles who have spent quite a few years obtaining skills

and a career often find themselves feeling self-sufficient. They maintain a social life, perhaps have bought a home and even do a little volunteer work. At some point even the successful single may admit that something is missing if he doesn't attend church. Another influential factor to drifting away from church may have been a childhood with an abundance of church activities and some degree of resentment.

My single career-minded daughter of the "baby boomer" era recently stated emphatically, "I was so sure I could make it on my own, but I'm admitting now that I need the support of my church. Life is too tough without it." She probably exemplifies many of her age group.

Changes of every kind have been exceedingly rapid throughout the 20th century. Add to that the life changes brought about when death and divorce occur and a chaotic situation may be inevitable. Support from a church can be significant.

In *The Pursuit of Happiness* Dr. Myers refers to studies which indicate that connections between religious faith and mental health are impressive. Religious people have less incidence of alcohol and drug abuse, are less delinquent, live longer, commit less suicide, have less incidence of mental illness, and are less apt to be divorced or unhappily married (142).

The value of "honest" (not pretentious) church affiliation must be important during times of life's changes and unexpected incidents (143). Dr.Myers suggests that a less than honest faith in anything might become "self-therapy," but he questions the value of such a vague spirituality. Faith in God does not promise an escape from suffering or stress, but it is linked with a strength during times of crisis. Life's changes bring about dark and dismal times, but people go through those changes alone only by choice (188).

Writer Og Mandino explains the spiritual needs of life this way. Mr. Mandino says that life need not be filled with religion in order to recognize a great mystery of nature. He points out that all creatures on earth including man, possess the instinct to cry for help. Mr. Mandino says that our cries are a form of prayer (105-106). Most people learn how to pray in church so that is another reason for attending.

Attending church alone, after having attended as a family unit is often extremely traumatic for the single person, but Dr. Myers explains that studies have been made concerning church attendance. He said that Gallup polls interviewing a cross-section of Americans show that people who were rated as highly spiritual and attended church also were twice as likely to say they were very happy.

Many denominations such as Baptists, Assembly groups, Methodists, Catholic, and Mormons, as well as Jewish Synogogues in some cities, have planned social events as well as Bible study and discussion groups for singles. Church-related singles retreats are held in various states and some on a nationwide basis. All these activities combine to help the singles understand and cope with their status in the world, whether it is by choice or by happenstance. Singles who have not been in a church group but are interested in being involved need to call their local church of preference to learn what is available.

Small towns and all churches have always frowned on divorce so it has been difficult for many churches to comprehend what should be done with the growing number of divorced single adults and now, the more rapidly growing number of never-married adults. In recent decades the percentage of singles in the total population has been near 40 percent, but the categories have changed. Now there are more never-married. As life-expectancy lengthens, the percentage of singles may increase.

Rachel now lives in an eastern city in the United States and has always been active in the Methodist church. Since her work has required her to move several times, she has been able to compare how different churches approach their single members. Some have had a very active single ministry and some have had none. She stated that although she likes her present church for other reasons, the ministry to singles is very weak. She declared that more than 50 percent of the church adult population is single, yet there is no distinct ministry to them, although the church is large enough to have other special ministries. Contrasting with that was a southwestern Methodist church which she attended a few years ago that had an extremely strong ministry to single adults. The explanation may lie in the attitude of the minister and the manner in which he leads the church concerning all special needs.

Today the First Baptist Church of Martha Lake (north of Seattle) assigns every member of the church to a deacon. The deacon is expected to keep in close touch with those to whom he is assigned. The deacon is available for budget counseling, emotional support and any way he can help. This program is very helpful to the singles in the church. My single daughters can testify to this. This is one of the examples of support available to singles in addition to game nights and group Bible study.

Both the new and old Testaments of the Bible contain inspirational words. Singles need to re-evaluate their reasons for attending or not attending church. Some find solace in reading the Scriptures but in addition to that, most find inspiration in hearing the Scriptures and the music usually associated with churches.

One writer explains one of the excuses for not attending church. Alla Bozarth-Campbell explains the common problem of being angry at God and blaming God for permitting us to suffer; or permitting the illness or death of a loved one. She says that the anger is a form of communication and its natural direction is outward, so raging against God can be healthy. She explains that clamming up is more damaging to a person of faith. Loss of faith is a devastating loss for one whose life has been shaped by belief. If this type of anger has become bottled up inside, that may be another reason to seek counseling or to allow the anger out so that reconciliation with God can be possible. A person who has had a strong belief can probably find the inspiration he needs in a church setting after a reconciliation with God takes place (3-5).

For all those who find themselves suddenly alone, the universal advice assuredly is: join a support group, find some new friends, and perhaps, become involved with a church of your choice, which can be another type of support group. It is also important that an optimistic person be on the list of good friends to help through tough times.

Finding moral support in single life can be an aid to adjusting attitudes, if that is necessary. A look at the possible need for attitude adjustment is considered in the next chapter.

FIVE
LIFE'S ATTITUDE ADJUSTMENTS

Certainly being married or single does not guarantee any specific attitudes will be present but very few make the change from married to single without some adjustments. A single-again person will probably have some attitude adjustments to make which often are more obvious to friends than the single person himself. Never-marrieds as well as other singles should examine their own attitudes to consider if they are appropriate in today's world.

ANGER

Anger is probably the least recognized of the emotions a person displays after a loss by divorce or death. Often people claim they are sad but their friends recognize many actions as being the result of anger.

Saint Augustine said "Anger is a weed" (Sermons 58) and no one likes weeds. However, anger is an appropriate emotion sometimes. If humans were incapable of anger they might never protect themselves from injustice or harm. If no one felt anger, injustices to the human race would go unpunished and ungoverned. Anger concerning unfairness has brought about the right to vote, child-labor laws, improved treatment in all labor conditions and numerous civil rights and educational laws in the United States. Without appropriate anger, discrimination of all kinds would never be corrected. It is the anger which turns into destructive rage and hostility that no one likes.

Wasting years being angry because a marriage ended in death or divorce may lead to physical illness. The anger can certainly reveal an attitude that wards off friends and does little, if any good. If you are having a difficult time adjusting to single life after a death or divorce, examine your attitudes. If you are angry, get over it. You are only hurting yourself.

Another specific time of anger may be when a person is using it to replace sorrow, oftentimes not quite aware of what is taking place. The acts of grieving might seem finished but another emotion may take its place, often anger.

In his book *Anger*, author Bill DeFoore explains that grieving is appropriate in both death and divorce (and many other losses). DeFoore also lists the stages of the grief process as he sees it: shock, denial, anger, guilt, pain and sorrow, release and resolution, and return to the willingness to love. He agrees that it is easy to get stuck in any part of the process, especially anger (13). The book deals with anger in all areas of life.

DeFoore says that stifling anger can be like an overheated pressure cooker, which will cause an internal explosion. This he explains usually means depression, self-hatred, major illness or all of the above. The healthy release of anger is needed for healing and recovery (13).

As proper use of anger plays such an important role in the recovery of all types of trauma including divorce and death, it should be carefully considered when previously married people cope with returning to the single world. It is easier to blame a specific act, person, or God as a cause of death or divorce than to accept them gracefully as one of life's changes or even possibly one's own fault.

It is true that many premature deaths and divorces could have been avoided. The divorce rate might drop if people did not jump into marriage without sufficient consideration of the matter. Other divorces could have been avoided by proper counseling. Many deaths are premature due to smoking, alcohol, and drug use. Many unwed mothers have lost a mate who "promised to be there" and perhaps had promised marriage. All losses require appropriate grieving. A loss must be dealt with, but when the incident is over it cannot be changed. Everyone must deal with the present and face the future. Seek counseling, if necessary. Do not continue in a state of anger.

Anger is not always a negative emotion, as DeFoore explains that anger can be your friend. He adds that anger is energy — emotional energy. It can turn into determination and motivation to get something done in spite of seemingly insurmountable odds. Take for example a person who has lifted an object of enormous weight to save a life, because he became angry at the fallen object (3). Stories abound of people who were fired or laid off from a job and were so angry they started their own businesses and often became millionaires.

I truly believe part of the reason I was able to complete college with five children in tow was due to anger. I was mad because the pastor of my church and the divorce attorney both told me I would have to give up going to school to support my children. They said I could expect very little child support. That was true so I went to school full-time and worked full-time. I had no savings and the only financial aid I found had to be repaid (which I welcomed, anyway). I was determined to gain skills for better jobs for two reasons. I wanted to prove it could be done and I needed to earn money to care for my children.

It is said that when we get angry, we feel physical changes. Our bodies are warm or hot, we feel tense, our hearts pound and certainly our thoughts race out of control. It is not a good time to try to communicate feelings. As anger lives within the body, not the brain, it must be released from the body (105). The simple little trick of counting to ten or naming books of the Bible used to help a lot of people relieve the tension they felt when they became angry, Reynolds Dodson says this is an angry age so those tricks may no longer suffice (185).

Part of the need to understand anger is gaining the ability to cope with other people's anger. If we have a single friend who expresses a lot of anger, perhaps we can help them understand why they are angry.

Because past incidents in life sometime trigger an angry reaction to a present situation, singles must take care not to release anger on someone who does not deserve it. In other words, being reminded of an ex-partner's habits or actions does not justify being angry at someone else. If this problem applies to you or a friend, try to resolve it.

If these suggestions are not sufficient, perhaps a self-help book devoted to anger management is appropriate. Internalized anger or rage developed from anger is not going to help single people cope with living in a double world. Those aspects of the emotional life need to be considered and dealt with or corrected. Now if singles could add a little patience to their lives perhaps the anger would go away.

Patience

"The strongest of all warriors are these two — Time and Patience"(Tolstoi X 16). Singles need an extra dose of patience and often an extra portion of time.

In more contemporary writing, businessman William B. Rouse includes patience as one of the three critical ingredients in discovery and life planning. The other two are persistence and passion. In the comments about patience, Rouse reminded that patience is needed because good things often take a lot of time, sometimes many years. The recovery from loss is a change. The adjustment to the change will require patience and time. Patience and time are necessary for all healing. Most psychologists as well as Mr. Rouse, seem to agree that the pain of loss won't last forever (38).

Intertwined with goal setting, life planning, and attitude adjustment is the need to allow time and to have patience for everything to come together in a sensible order. Emotions can be managed, but recognizing the source of each emotion and using it appropriately is a learning process. Remember Mandino's admonition to be the master of your emotions (89).

In *LIFE IS GOODBYE/LIFE IS HELLO*, Ms. Alla Bozarth-Campbell said not to be alarmed or surprised if your attitude toward yourself and others is changed. It may be altered for the better. Ms. Bozarth-Campbell also explained how emotional pain can be transferred to the body and become a real physical illness when it cannot otherwise be expressed (67-71). Unfortunately, Americans have less tolerance for psychological recovery than physical recovery. Sympathy for physical illness is easier to get than sympathy for sadness. And what does this have to do with patience? Some may describe patience as the ability to wait. Waiting and finding appropriate ways to pass time are necessary to the healing process of grief.

Ms. Bozarth-Campbell encourages talking to trusted friends or relatives so that they know about the loss and its meaning. She says that another therapeutical measure is to keep a journal. She advises recording all secret feelings and impressions, doubts and fears, and hopes and longings. She claims a journal is a journey toward healing and renewal, an active act of learning to wait and be patient for the healing to take place (46).

While you are grieving, you are in the process of restoring your basic capacity for life. During a time of healing you won't experience great joys or intense pleasures. This is a good time to develop a new appreciation for the simple gifts of life.

Nothing is more healing than water. With the nation-wide development of many recreational spots, most people are close to water, even if it is a small lake or pond. If not, alternate suggestions include swimming, having an aquarium or imagining a shower as a waterfall. For many people, walking can aid in the healing process. Because so much happens so rapidly in the technology developed in the 20th century, many Americans may have lost the ability to be patient. We must remember that many worthwhile accomplishments take time.

"This too shall pass" is an attitude of patience. Og Mandino says patience will carry people through adversity and maintain balance in life (94). Balance in life not only includes patience but also includes a bit of defiance and stubbornness.

Defiant or Stubborn?

When is it good to be defiant or stubborn? Perhaps when the world has made false assumptions about a single person's ability or characteristics, it is time to prove the world wrong. Many a success story rings with the sound of stubbornness — an attitude of "don't give up."

When Bessie Pender made a failing grade after returning to college she could have given up, but a younger sister encouraged her to be stubborn and go on with her life-time dream. She did and after being a janitor's assistant for seventeen years, Pender finished college and became a fifth grade teacher (Slack 78).

Single parents have to employ a degree of stubbornness as well as hard work in order to defy the statistics surrounding the lives of children in single parent homes. Single parents who make extra effort to take care of physical, educational and emotional needs of their children can reap rewards. Those families must have an "it doesn't matter, we can do it" attitude.

Success stories of children raised by single parents abound. David Belton's mother supported her six children by cleaning houses, yet today Mr. Belton is an attorney in Columbia, S.C. (Slack 77). Even President Bill Clinton was raised by a single mom. The stories of successful people who were raised by a single parent are not uncommon.

Being stubborn as in not giving up, is a healthy trait, but being stubborn as in not considering another's viewpoint, is usually a detriment in relationships. Stubbornness in the male-oriented culture of the United States, especially during most of the 20th century, created many of the problems involving widowed and divorced women who had no salable skills.

When I first married I had completed one year of college and always wanted to finish. We moved very close to an inexpensive teacher's college where I could have easily finished and obtained a teacher's certificate. That was one time I should have been much more defiant than I was, because when I found myself with an unwanted divorce my salable skills were limited.

Writer Pat Hudson admonishes that it is all right to choose to be a homemaker as a career but that all should use some of the time to get prepared—just in case (142). I believe her advice is appropriate because no one has any way of knowing what will happen later in life. She was referring to gaining skills to use later in life when children are grown or in the event of loss of spouse for any reason. Many a husband's disabling accident has also caused a formerly secure woman to return to the work force. Most of us do not live on a farm or have a situation in which we just "take over the business" without much training. Nor are very many families so financially well-off that the loss of parent is not a handicap in many ways.

Let an attitude of defiance rule, only if it is necessary for achieving well thought out goals that will better life's situation. It may be difficult to admit, but sometimes two is better than one, as is discussed next.

Two is Better Than One - Many Times

For the stubborn never-married or the upset widow or widower and the recently divorced people who may all have an "I can do it by myself" attitude, a little flexibility may be necessary. I used to have a T-Shirt that read "The Best Man for the Job is a Woman." I have seen one that purports "A Woman Needs a Man Like a Fish Needs a Bicycle." Although I am extremely self-sufficient and independent, I will admit that two is often better than one. A little help reaching things, planting trees and fixing the roof is great.

Being independent and self-reliant may be admirable, but being too defiant and stubborn may not be a desirable trait. If you are defiant and stubborn you may lie injured in the grass unnoticed because of a fall, when you should have waited until someone could help you install that needed yard light. At times, it is appropriate to ask for help or at least let someone know your plans in the event you don't show up for work one day or answer the telephone at an appointed time! It is difficult for those who have become self-reliant because of adversities in life to admit they could use a little help physically or emotionally.

Common sense should not be replaced by stubbornness or any other characteristic. The attitude "I didn't think" is no excuse if a person wants to live a long and healthy life. "I just did it one time" is also no substitute for wisdom. According to statistics, most accidents are due to human error.

Occasionally, while I lived in Washington (the state), I was a little 'carried away' in my defiant, 'I can do it' attitude. At my place (isolated in the country, by the way) was a very old, lone cherry tree, part of an original orchard long gone. The cherries were ripe and no one was available to observe me on the ladder picking the cherries. It was an orchard ladder. It was sturdy but as is typical with ladders, they seem to incite accidents. One moment I was picking cherries, and the next minute my foot missed the ladder step and I went to the ground. Fortunately, it was not an extremely tall ladder, so the fall bruised my dignity more than my body. It was a reminder though as to the possibilities of being on the ground, hurt and unnoticed for a long time, possibly days.

The brain is a body part made for thinking and every person living alone should be alert to the problems of being alone. They must stop and think "Should I do this alone or should I wait until I have a little help?"

Locked In or Locked Out?

Do you sometimes feel locked out from others and that they have kept their true feelings locked in? In *Listen to the Heart* Roberta Meyer explains intimacy. Many of us need lessons on this subject. Intimacy is allowing others to make themselves known to you, while you are revealing your innermost self to them.

Communication is the first implication of intimacy, yet Ms. Meyer reminds that immediate communication does not mean revealing every thought or feeling that crosses the mind. We have to learn to create opportunities for timely and appropriate communication (12).

The life situations created by unexpected or unwelcome divorce and death often add to a person's inability to communicate. The anger, disappointment and sometimes guilt experienced in those situations may cause the distressed to stifle emotions and be locked in to an unhappy, unrewarding, and unproductive life. In On a Clear Day You Can See Yourself Dr. Sonya Friedman warns of being locked in by bitterness. When trust has been destroyed in a relationship or marriage, it does not have to apply to everyone else of the opposite sex from that day forward. Building a life of being able to trust again can be pursued in small steps, just as other aspects of recovery must be approached slowly (173-176).

Any ability that is damaged must be repaired gradually. When nerves damage the spine and a person has to learn to walk again, he does not begin with a three mile hike. He takes one step at a time. Why is the concept of rebuilding a life after divorce or death so hard for so many to comprehend? Life is full of detours, mistakes, and surprises. It is up to each individual to deal with them according to his ability and desires. When people see a detour in a roadway, some might know an alternate route other than the guided detour. Neither do individuals handle life's detours the same way.

Friends cannot be much help if the emotionally hurt person locks in all his feelings and in turn, locks out all the warmth and friendliness offered to him.

Do You Need an Attitude Adjustment?

As single people we generally seem to agree that many in the double world need an attitude adjustment concerning the single lifestyle. On the other hand let us be careful of our own attitudes. Sometimes we may appear to ask for sympathy when the world feels it has offered enough. Sometimes we complain about our problems when those in the double world have other problems but don't complain. Although we have problems unique to the single world we have no monopoly on problems. We should not assume or act as though married people have no problems.

We need to assert ourselves in a positive, happy manner that lets others know that sometimes life alone is quite different but as humans we have the same thoughts and abilities that married people do. Several years ago the people of our nation were encouraged to bridge the generation gap through better communication. We now need to bridge the gap between singles and married people the same way.

With our attitudes adjusted we will be in better position to consider life's goal posts as discussed in the next chapter.

SIX
LIFE'S GOAL POSTS

Many incidents in life can make us stop and realize we need to set some goals. Any or all of these could cause us to consider making some goals: a change in status (married to single), an admission that nothing will change (forever single), a recognition of an unfulfilling lifestyle (alcohol or drugs) or a sudden awakening to the fact that we have no goals.

Time for Self-analysis

The first step in goal setting will be an analysis of abilities, problems and achievements. In *Positive Plus*, Dr. Joyce Brothers, herself now a widow, gives specific guidelines in self-analysis. She suggests that we ask ourselves these four things: are we on the right track, are we making the most of ourselves, are we getting what we want out of life and are we happy (11-12).

Dr. Brothers said that if you answer "No" to even one of these questions, you are getting a bum deal out of life. She claims that 99 percent of the people who feel this way can usually turn their lives around by making one or two small changes in their attitudes or behaviors. She also insists that everyone usually knows their own traits and which need to be improved. Dr. Brothers adds that no one is perfect, but that everyone can change and learn to control bad traits (12-13).

Dr. Brothers explains that a behavior as simple as yelling at the kids can be changed. She says that children are so used to it, they don't listen. However, if the yelling is restrained to once a month, they very well may perk up, take notice and listen to the command. The book is a gold mine about pinpointing self-defeating traits and changing them (*Positive Plus*).

John Gardner was Secretary of Health, Education and Welfare under President Lyndon Johnson and most recently a professor at Stanford University. He has written several books and recently said that in order to renew our lives after change or loss we must be interested in things outside of self. We must keep a sense of curiosity and discover new things (The Futurist, 9-12).

He also explains in his article the many ways people learn and that learning should never stop. Similar to what Brothers teaches, Gardner states that we need to learn NOT to engage in self-destructive behavior. We should NOT burn up energy in anxiety and we should learn how to manage our tensions. Gardner insists that self-pity and resentment are among the most toxic of drugs. He also said that we need to understand that most people are neither for you nor against you; they are thinking about themselves (9-12).

Make a list of your behaviors and attitudes. Consider everything from speech to budget, mannerisms and personality traits. What needs to be changed? No psychologist, including Dr. Brothers, recommends trying to change every bad habit all at once. It is also not necessary to see a psychologist to correct every bad or self-defeating habit. Group therapy may be especially helpful in some cases, such as: TOPS (Take Off Pounds Sensibly), Weight Watchers, and Alcoholics Anonymous. These all offer group support for correcting eating and drinking habits. Some churches now offer plans such as First Place or Weigh Down that incorporate spiritual guidance and motivation for weight control.

Examining one's habits, attributes, and problems must also include a look at job status and career goals. Singles who find themselves in new situations because of divorce or death sometimes need to "regroup." As Collin Perry states in "Help Yourself Through the Hard Times," a new situation is the time to plan events and learn new skills (125). Even if the new skill is just a hobby, it can be a help in readjusting to a new life.

Daydreams Can Become Goals

Daydreams and goals are similar. Many times a goal follows a daydream. I would like to tell you about my daydreams and goals but let me also tell you about some others whose paths have crossed my life and whose lives and examples influenced me. As I was in the middle of working on my goal to finish college I worked part time for a newspaper. That work allowed my introduction to the first two people described here. The accomplishments listed are not because of being single but all were single at the time of the accomplishments.

Fred Newton, who lived in Clinton, Oklahoma, during the 1920s, dreamed of swimming down the Mississippi River. Fred's dream was a little outlandish for someone who lived in what would soon become part of the dust bowl. The town did not even have a swimming pool. Fred made his dream a goal while he was a single young man. It took a couple of years before he accomplished the feat in 1930. It is doubtful he would have had such a goal if he had the responsibility of a family and considering the economy of the United States at that time.

Another person I met was Edna Gardner Whyte. She was a registered nurse who dreamed of flying. She obtained her pilot's license in 1926 and began a long career of flying and instructing. She overcame many obstacles to fulfill each of her dreams. She was single and alone, being ridiculed by men when she learned to fly (Very few women were pilots in 1926.) She loved to race in the air and had a large trophy case with proof of her ability.

Edna later married, but was divorced and alone again when she tried to fulfill another dream, that of owning a small airport. When men in county government insisted she could not fulfill her dream of building an airport she defiantly went about doing it. She had no financial backing except her ability to instruct. Her airport was a 'pay as you go' project. When she sold her airport near Denton, Texas, it brought more than a million dollars. Today the Aero-Valley Airport still sports fly-ins and serves the purpose Edna intended.

Later on I was editing newspapers in North Central Washington when a young man named Rob Sweetgall came walking through the towns which housed my newspapers on two separate occasions. Rob grew up in Brooklyn and learned to be a chemical engineer. During the 12 years he worked for DuPont he once heard a professor speak about cardiovascular risk factors at a safety meeting. He had already become a triathlete-marathoner. He said he became such a fitness fanatic that in 1981 he quit his DuPont job, knowing he wanted to be a health-fitness something. He said he had heard his colleagues talk about their dreams which would require leaving behind their security. Rob was a bachelor and said that if he had his health that was the only security he needed.

Rob did not know at first what he wanted to do until he decided if he could be half the speaker the professor was, he could walk around America and tell school children about exercise, especially walking. Rob has done that several times. His business is now called Creative Walking, from whose headquarters he flies to speaking engagements, promotes walking with videos, books, and journals. Rob is on a mission, which is his goal, to help more people understand cardiovascular fitness to avoid early deaths.

Not all who dream and accomplish goals become famous or make the history books. A lot of goals are reached quietly but affect many lives in a positive way. Alice* was a factory worker in a small town in Washington. She dreamed of caring for disabled children and adults in her home. She set a goal, planned, obtained the license, quit her factory job, and now has realized her dream.

I never stopped dreaming of a college education. The dream became a goal, but not before I had five children. Just as I started classes a divorce was unavoidable. Attending classes after transporting children to schools and sitters can be accomplished. Willpower must be strong. Sometimes sacrifice, sometimes taking risks, usually very hard work and lots of patience are required to make dreams come true.

All of these stories, including mine, are book-length with their details. They all had similar characteristics, in that hard work, perseverence and patience were involved. Many people have worth-while dreams and goals but give up because they run out of patience.

In *Solution Oriented Woman*, Pat Hudson named several things such as taking on a tough project as requiring the ability to daydream success. Ms. Hudson, W. Clement Stone and Napoleon Hill all claim that what the mind can conceive and believe, it can achieve (see bibliography). In other words you must have the ability to daydream success.

Action must be taken in order for dreams to become goals and then accomplishments. It is easy to get lost in a comfort zone of life and never try anything new. A dream will never become a goal and a goal will never become a reality in a comfort zone.

Some people never stay in a comfort zone very long and others never leave theirs. Anthony* was an architect who lived in and was educated in Texas. He loved to camp and see the outdoors but he was afraid to go to a new location to pursue work. He was not a risk taker. He stayed in his comfort zone. He never knew what he might have accomplished, had he taken a risk and gone to a different location.

George* was a farmer and so was his brother. George was an excellent farmer, whose farm was viewed by county farm agents on tours every year. George's brother Harry* bought land and farmed. Harry added to his farm through the years. He built storage silos, bought equipment and built a nice house. He was considered successful but his farm was not as immaculate and exemplary as George's farm. The main problem with George's farm was that it was on rented land, because George was always afraid to buy land. George also was afraid to marry; so he when he grew old, he found himself alone and almost penniless because he would never take a chance or dream a dream.

Of course many dreamers have no idea how to begin to realize their hopes, to turn their dreams into goals and ultimately successes. In *Do It*, Peter McWilliams and John-Roger suggest using 3 X 5 cards to make lists. Headings can be devised according to your dreams. List in simple terms your desires, abilities and financial needs or other concerns. Itemizing dreams or wants in a realistic manner and looking at the choices and consequences can aid in planning (225).

McWilliams and John-Roger remind that when choices are made, winning is not always assured but neither is losing. They proclaim that everyone is worthy and has a special dream. Everyone has his own power to help make dreams come true. These authors also point out that many people try to rationalize that money is the reason for not doing something they want to do (235). The example of writing a book is cited. A pencil, a tablet and fifteen minutes a day are what is necessary to write a book — not an expensive computer.

McWilliams and John-Roger are among a host of authors who insist the important step in fulfilling dreams is to *Do It* and do it now (371). Dreams will never get past the front door without action.

Never Say Too Late

Never say you are too old or that you have too many children to care for or any other excuse you might conjure to keep you from doing something you have always longed to do. If you discover a new dream later in life, let it become a possibility. If you have no friends to encourage you, find some inspirational books such as *Sometimes We Dance Alone* or *Do It* to boost your morale.

Michelle* was a single parent who had been on welfare and was certainly not happy with her status in life but she was fortunate to make a new friend who was an optimist. Unfortunately, Michelle's own family had never encouraged her to pursue a different life. She had artistic talents and the new friend Anita*, helped her find the financial aids she needed to go to college and prepare herself for the job world.

Michelle finished her college work though it took a little longer than four years. She was even able to participate in a study in Europe. Now Michelle has made a place for herself in the work world. She not only had thought it was too late but would never have pursued the change had she listened to her parents and siblings. Her friend encouraged her all the way to the finish.

Edna Whyte was past sixty when she opened Aero-Valley Airport. She continued to teach flying until she was past 80 when cataract surgery prohibited it. John Gardner took a new job at 76. Bob Dole was past 70 when he ran for president. "Too late" is usually an attitude, not a fact.

Goals For Survival or a Better Life

Learning to set goals is part of every motivational and self-improvement course or seminar, whether it is involved in sales or therapy. Goals can involve all facets of life: physical, mental, emotional, and spiritual.

In his article for The Futurist John Gardner explained how life is constantly unfolding and, if we wish it to be, an endless process of self-discovery. Mr. Gardner said that we can continually carry on a dialogue between our own potentialities and the life situations in which we find ourselves. He insists that for renewal, a tough-minded optimism is best. Mr. Gardner also said that if we want to shape the future we must believe in the future (12).

Goals are achievements to be accomplished in the future. It is the purpose of any plan or action — an aim or end. One of the messages in Mr. Mandino's story about the greatest salesman on earth is to increase your worth every day by a hundredfold (95). If that seems an impractical or impossible goal, consider the rest of the message. Mr. Mandino points out that the genius of man can create silk from a mulberry leaf, can create a castle from a field of clay, and can make a sheep's hair into clothing for a king. Mr. Mandino asks if leaves and clay and hair can have their value multiplied a hundred or a thousandfold by men, isn't it probable that we could do the same with our own selves? (97). We all know that a grain of wheat will grow into a stalk which will multiply a hundedfold and those grains will feed many people. Why do we think ourselves less valuable than wheat?

Every motivational workshop or seminar I've attended has made it clear that we must learn to set goals for the day, the week, the year and life. Mr. Mandino's teachings are in accordance with that but he added that it is important to announce goals to others. In so doing we publicly acknowledge that we have made goals and even if they have to be modified, that is all right. Letting others know our goals helps us learn to be accountable.

Mr. Gardner said that life's challenges keep coming and keep changing. New goals and new aims are a part of a new life, especially after major life changes such as death or divorce. Gardner suggests that goals are not necessarily a change of direction — they may be necessary for doing a better job at whatever you're already doing. To some, goal-setting may be the only way to plan for a better future. Again Gardner emphasized tough-minded optimism.No one ever promised that life would be easy — and yes, bad things happen to good people. It is also all right to fail as long as you remember to try again (12).

Krystal is my youngest daughter who has a pre-school child. Krystal is 30 and her life corresponds with many of the statistics of the 1990s. She had her child by choice, vowed to be off welfare long before the mandate, lives alone and has more than one salable skill. For a couple of years she has dreamed of operating a somewhat unique business. She has worked sufficiently to have Earned Income Credit (Income Tax) and is using that to finalize her business plan. She plans to do a cosmetology business by taking the service to those in need. Krystal has done a lot of preparation to come to this stage in her plan. She researched to learn about all the licenses needed, contacted agencies concerning her idea, has a part time job for "base income" and is ready to go.

My oldest daughter Cynthia returned to school to learn more about the photography which had become her part time business. Cynthia's back injury as a nurse and subsequent surgeries caused her to pursue the new work, which she hopes will be full time as she recovers. Cynthia and Krystal are good examples of those who make goals of their dreams, which in turn is a builder of self-esteem.

Automatic Esteem Builders

In *How to Raise Your Self Esteem*, Nathaniel Branden says that how people feel about themselves affects every aspect of their experience. That includes the way they function at work, at play, and the way they act as parents, as well as how they achieve in life. In his opinion, self-esteem is the key to success or failure. Certainly, it is an important factor (5).

In a recent bulletin from the Skyline Urban Ministries of Oklahoma City, Irene, the person in charge of the clothing room, thanked specific people who had left name labels in the clothes they had donated. Irene was thanking them, while admitting she did not know them. She told how various ones had come for help and been given nice clothes to wear to job interviews. Self-esteem can be raised by dressing nicely. Irene also expressed appreciation for all the nameless donors who help brighten the lives of others.

In the event you have not discovered this, it is correct that you feel good when you do good for others. Feeling good is one step in raising your self-esteem. So if you feel a little less successful than you think you should, try doing some acts of one-to-one volunteering. You will feel better about yourself.

Occasionally each of us needs to be reminded that we are special and that God has a place for each of us. One of the scrolls in *The Greatest Salesman in the World* reminds us that we are nature's greatest miracle. We are unique creatures. As each person is unique and the only one with his or her special characteristics and attributes, he or she must utilize his own abilities (81-82).

Rejection, guilt, grief and depression must be dealt with in order to move on in life. The thing to do after a good self-analysis is to put the new goals and plans into motion. As each small goal is accomplished, self-esteem will grow.

Self-esteem should not be measured in clothes sizes or physical fitness. Psychologists all emphasize that people must first like themselves in order to raise their self-esteem. If weight is a serious (as in health) problem, get help. Certainly self-esteem is improved by a healthier, more average body appearance for both men and women. Studies show that men and women are both caught up in the pursuit of thinness because of the pressures of the culture. The fact that obesity lowers self-esteem and creates depression is of growing concern in the United States. Everyone needs to learn that thin is rarely possible and rarely healthy (Brothers 74).

Dr. Brothers says that women especially, are more concerned over the "ideal body" than they should be. She gave an example of a short, slightly pudgy woman who is also pretty. Dr. Brothers noted that the chubby woman seems to light up the room when she walks in, because of her smile. Her size had nothing to do with her winning smile (75).

After a good self-analysis and some goal-setting, it is time to take action. Acting upon the new plans will do a lot to raise self-esteem. As Gardner insists, nothing is easy, life constantly changes and challenges, but that may be why it is worth living, even when single in a double world (11).

Setting goals to fulfill dreams is an important task, especially for single people who are taking charge of their lives, but paying attention to the financial aspects of living is also important. A lot of facts have emerged concerning singles and their finances which will be discussed in the next chapter.

SEVEN

LIFE'S DOLLAR SIGNS

Census reports are helpful in revealing how many people are never married and all the other numbers about the single population, but it is difficult to determine which problems in money management are most unique to singles. A great majority of single parents have some money problems, if one is to believe any reports at all. It does seem obvious that most single parent families are concerned with income and/or how to save and plan for the future. According to many recent magazine articles, a great number of singles do not plan their finances wisely. This chapter will address some of those facts including bartering, how to cut back on expenses and how to enjoy some free and nearly free things in life.

Learn to Barter

Bartering is an age-old practice of trading goods and services without the use of money; the practice has never gone out of style. As singles are often stretched for both time and money they can learn to barter among friends and colleagues. When singles need to tackle a big job and do not have the resources, perhaps a little bartering will spell success. According to an article in *Kiplinger's Personal Finance Magazine* many businesses save cash by bartering. It makes sense to apply the same philosophy to the individual world, specifically singles (Roha 103-104).

While singles may not say, "You move my company; I'll print your brochures," they often say, "You help me move this weekend; I'll throw a big pizza party when we finish." The same thing is possible with single parents who often exchange baby-sitting chores. Of course, agreements need to be clear so that hard feelings are avoided. Exchanging babysitting is one category of bartering which could easily be abused. Keep it fair, if you do it.

Opportunities for bartering are another result of networking in an active support group. Members of support groups can promote bartering throughout their group: everything from minor car tune-ups to pet-sitting to hairdos to lawn mowing.

My daughter Krystal is a single parent in Everett, Washington, who is a licensed barber. She often does haircuts in exchange for minor car upkeep (she furnishes the supplies) or for a lawn mowing. While my mother was a widow in Oklahoma City she didn't go out much but still drove her car. She did some pet-sitting for her neighbor who owned a garage. She was sure he never charged her the full price on her car repairs and pet-sitting was one way she could repay the family when they travelled. She also did mending for another neighbor who in turn, pruned her rose bushes each year.

If the widow in a support group is the only one with a house and a big yard, she can offer her location for a yard sale. Single guys in apartments can offer to mow yards in exchange for the niceties of home-cooked meals. Support groups can maintain on-going lists of jobs and ideas for bartering.

Bartering ideas will vary according to the population and the geographic location. Singles in Washington state won't be looking for help to batten down for an oncoming hurricane nor will a Floridian be looking for someone to shovel snow.

John*, a divorced man in Port Lavaca, Texas, who has lived alone for many years, enjoys doing things for other single friends. He loans one of his vehicles if a friend's has a break down. He will gladly install a yard light or a new mailbox and at the same time, he always welcomes homemade cookies and a visit over a cup of coffee. Bartering is not meant to be complicated. Single friends may not even think of it as "bartering." Rather, they may view these exchanges as just being helpful.

Exchanging vacation homes might be considered a form of bartering. The networking that is a result of a support or special interest group might very well create friendships that would allow some travel together. Home exchanging for vacations has grown in popularity in recent years. A handbook is available: *Trading Places* by Bill and Mary Barbour. Obviously, exchanging homes is a good way to learn about another part of the country as well as a means of saving dollars (Dienstag, Nov 1996).

Indeed, there are many possibilities when considering travelling with one or more other persons. Having a same sex travelling companion may be a good idea, especially if one or the other is not confident enough to travel alone. Travelling in pairs also cuts car and motel expenses. Singles, who are usually on a tighter budget than married couples, should join a group such as American Association of Retired Persons (AARP) as soon as they are eligible. AARP now invites members at age 50 and even inexpensive motels, such as MOTEL 6, offer discounts for AARP or Triple A members.

Two very new books for solo travelers are *Traveling Solo* by Eleanor Berman and *Travel Alone and Love It* by Sharon Wingler. The first has advice and ideas for more than 250 vacations. The latter is a flight attendant's guide to solo travel. They are only published as this is written. Perhaps they will even be in your library by the time you read this. They are recommended by "*The Hartford Courant*" newspaper's travel editor (June, 1997).

The Best Things in Life are Free

With the age of costly toys and personal computers and big screen digital televisions have come generations of people who may have forgotten that many things in life are free. It is not too late to use that philosophy, especially if one is on a tight budget. If a single person—or single parent family—has made a firm resolution to begin saving, they can also enjoy some of the things in life that are free and bolster the savings program.

There are activities and pasttimes in life that are free. First, consider these free visual treats. When the sun shines on a field of snow, it creates an illusion of diamonds in the snow. When the sun and rain cooperate in a certain way, a double rainbow can form. Of course any rainbow is beautiful. For years children have had fun giving names to cloud formations. What is more beautiful than a peacock spreading its tail feathers? It doesn't take much space to install some kind of bird feeder so that birds of the season can be observed. Almost everyone is amazed at the variety of snowflake patterns observed when snowflakes are caught on black paper.

If you stop and listen, the earth is plentiful with sounds for which there is no charge. Wind in the top of tall pine trees makes a special sound as does snow crunching under boots. Soft rain on the roof is almost as tranquilizing as waves hitting a seashore. A mockingbird's song can hold an audience as well as an expensive concert. A baby's first laugh is a priceless sound. Thunder, especially if it is a rare sound, as in the Pacific Northwest, is actually fun to hear. Those who live in such a region sometimes purchase cassette tapes or CDs in order to listen to thunder and falling rain. (North Central Washington has little of either.) Often school and community concerts are free. Some small towns have musical groups performing in the town square on special occasions. Many churches have special musical performances, not only at Christmas and Easter, but at other times throughout the year. Although offerings may be taken, most have no requirement for contributions. No offering was taken for my church's production of the *Living Christmas Tree* last year. It is considered a service to the community.

Those who are blind or have hearing problems usually develop an acute sense of touch. The hearing and seeing world would do well to cultivate an awareness of that sense. A baby's soft skin, a firm handshake, or a cool shower after a hot summer day are keen reminders of the ability to feel. Try being aware of wet sand on bare feet, the moss on a rock or log, or the warmth of a furry kitten. Holding a hand can acknowledge the chemistry of the phenomenon of love or comfort a sick person. Hands can feel the smoothness of a carefully sanded board, as well as the softness of certain cloth materials.

The human life is usually blessed with the ability to smell lilacs in bloom, an apple orchard ready to harvest, or a pine forest. Fresh-turned dirt, ready to plant flowers and vegetables is an odor not only reserved for a farmer. And who has never noticed the smell of an approaching rain? A planned trip to the nearest rural area may be richer in rewards than winning a lottery ticket. In such a place, the sights, sounds and odors of the world are unrestrained and available without a fee. In a truly remote area, one can listen to the quiet and observe with all the senses, and probably return home refreshed and ready to greet another day.

Single parents often feel rushed because of double responsibilities and frustrated because of insufficient income. The same free activities are available today as were available fifty years ago, but most parents seem to have forgotten they exist. It is still possible to find a clover patch and look for a "lucky" four-leaf clover. Both boys and girls can play dress-up with their parents' clothes, shoes, or hats. Children could still play marbles on a dirt mound, if they were instructed, and they could make roads and hills in the dirt for toy cars. Do children know about lightning bugs and that they can be put in a jar?

Free and near free activities usually take more effort than money. While I was teaching in a small west Texas town, I still had three children under twelve at home (two others were in college). One day I told them they could invite some friends to go along to look for wild flowers. Permission was gained from the other parents.

A forty mile mile round trip in the back roads allowed lots of flower picking as well as fun in the real outdoors. The trip ended in a very small village that had a former old saloon converted into a drug store. The children all thought sitting on the bar stools for a cold drink was very exciting. No one was bored or complained on the virtually free excursion. Perhaps every single parent reading this can come up with a lot of good ideas. The trip only cost a couple of gallons of gas and a few soda pops. It was an afternoon outing, not all day. Children do not have to be entertained with costly items.

A city-bound single parent might recommend going to a McDonald's or similar fast food place with play equipment to spend some inexpensive time. A cup of coffee or a soft drink for the parent allows children unlimited play time in a confined area. The parent does not have as much space to monitor as in a public park.

Singles, especially if they are history buffs, should remember that alert elderly citizens have extremely interesting stories to tell and certainly never charge the listener! A visit to an elderly friend or neighbor or even in a nursing home can bring many unexpected rewards.

The single population would do well to remember that money cannot buy happiness and perhaps some of the best things in life are free. In her book, *Positive Plus*, Dr. Brothers reminds us that money is not all-powerful. Too many people believe that if they had enough money, they would be happy. Money will not fulfill emotional needs or supply what is lacking in our lives. Having money will not improve our self-esteem. To believe that having money will cure all problems is self-defeating and will lead to trouble, according to Dr. Brothers (106-107).

Professional Advice is Usually Best

Several authors and financial writers advocate professional advice concerning money, especially when a person becomes single by death or divorce. Rae Lindsey, in *Alone and Surviving*, recounts ways that various friends and relatives offer financial advice to the newly single person. Her best advice, after suffering consequences of what she considered bad advice, is to seek professional help (89-104). Money and finances should not be played with like a Monopoly game, but it is crucial for singles to get their financial picture in order.

Tracey Longo's article in a 1996 issue of "*Kiplinger's Personal Finance Magazine*", indicates that many singles need help in planning finances. The average single (includes both men and women) earns *LESS THAN HALF* the amount of the average income earned by married couples. (Do not ask me to explain why that is true; this is from a reputable magazine.) Statistics also reveal that a greater percentage of married couples save for retirement than do singles over 21. The article also cites evidence why two can live more cheaply than one. The reference in two living cheaper applies to operating a household. Simple arithmetic explains the costs of mortgage or rent as being double if in two houses. The article emphasizes the importance for singles to begin intelligent financial planning for the future (81-83).

The choices of where to go for financial planning have also increased in recent years. Most people have checking accounts at a bank, yet my banker said that very few bank customers use the bank for financial planning, which is available. Investment firms have a financial planner who will guide the investor and explain all the possibilities.

Some attorneys specialize in wills and trusts, and there is a considerable difference in the two. Singles should ask a friend to explain the difference, or seek help at the library first. Perhaps then a single would be ready to discuss the difference with planner. Singles should become informed whether they have a large estate or not. Only a few single people have absolutely no heirs.

As for buying a house, many singles are still unaware that there are many ways of financing property. Tracey Longo states that one helpful means is getting a mortgage with no money down. As home prices vary a great deal from one coast to the other and all the towns and cities in between, singles should seek out real estate offices that will lead them to the many options now available in house financing. Depending on the geographic location, monthly mortgage payments may be lower than rent for the same type of dwelling in many parts of the United States. So even though the single might have little equity in a house, if the payment is less than rent, it will develop an equity in time.

Evelyn* found herself divorced in a west coast state, far from her childhood home. She knew the property values were much lower in the southwest than on the west coast. She also knew she could never afford to own a house if she stayed on the coast. She asked her company, a national insurance company, for a transfer to her home state. She felt that owning a home was important as part of a long-range investment and retirement plan.

Evelyn went to a real estate office in the new location and was guided to a home she could well afford on her modest income. The mortgage payment is about one-half the rental cost for comparable property in her former residence. Moving may not be easy but the long-range financial advantage may be worth it. Eveyln realistically considered her probability of remarriage and planned for her future as a single person.

Marriage and children can't always be planned but a person has a better chance with finances. Many funds (mutual, etc.) allow a sign up with no minimum investment, if a person agrees to have $50 or more a month automatically invested from a checking account (*Consumer Report* 1995). Almost every financial planner should have information on that type of investment.

Singles may not need much life insurance or none at all if they have a savings or burial plan. However, according to Longo's article disability insurance is critical. For years the insurance industry has estimated that one out of four adults will be disabled for at least three months before they reach 65. Only about 40 percent of U.S. workers have enough insurance through employers to replace 60% of their income (83). So when a nationally recognized company's sales person comes knocking at the door to explain disability insurance, it will be wise to listen.

When a seminar or workshop is available on estate planning, financial planning or budgeting, take advantage. This is not the 19th century when pioneers dug a grave, placed a marker and simply divided the belongings of the deceased. It is not absolutely necessary to consult a professional financial planner, but it has become imperative to do financial planning with or without help.

Yes, You Can Adjust Your Budget

Tracey Longo's "*Painless Ways to Tame Your Spending*" reveals that getting fiscal religion may be as easy as coveting a ski trip. He says to set a goal, face up to your spending, pinpoint what you can do without and make saving effortless (91-92).

When a goal is set, post a picture of the car or house or vacation or college degree or retirement home out in the open, where it is always clearly visible. For most of us, it is best to make a few realistic goals on the way to a larger goal. As one goal is accomplished, we should add to our list.

When changing a financial lifestyle as in other life changes, it is usually better to make little changes gradually. New goals can be added as progress is made. A habitual movie-goer would not be expected to change the pattern of movie attendance abruptly. However, reducing attendance from twice a week to once a week is a substantial savings. Make realistic goals.

Past spending *MUST* be reviewed and analyzed before any changes can be made. Old check registers and credit card statements should be totaled in order to summarize your spending habits. Add all miscellaneous spending that is not a controlled item (such as rent/mortgage, utilities, regular monthly payments) for a twelve month period and divide by twelve to see what your monthly average is. You could separate groceries and eating out in one category. When that is done you should have a better picture of your spending habits. This is similar to a doctor ordering a person to make a list of everything eaten in a given time. Putting it on paper and looking at it is an awakening. When you see how you have spent, you will know what to consider for change.

Cash that was spent and is not accounted for should prompt serious thinking. Do *NOT* assume where your money goes unless you are already on a strict budget which you do follow. For example if every week you retain $25 in cash for coffee breaks and miscellaneous for which you do not want to write checks, can you account for most of that money? The issue here is not an attempt to deny you some miscellaneous spending, just that miscellaneous spending can be overdone the same as any other habit.

Now that you have summarized your spending, analyze it. Is too much of your income going for credit card interest or overdraft fees? Does gift giving appear overly generous? How about lottery tickets or Bingo or other gambling devices? With the increased cost of tobacco usage, let alone the increased health risk warnings, surely every smoker would do his or her health and pocketbook a favor by cutting down or stopping the use of tobacco. The same is true with alcohol; a regular casual drinker might save a substantial sum by sipping only one drink wherever he socializes, especially if he stops on the way home every night. Every person's spending habits are different. Every individual must examine his own spending in order to correct any problems. *THE BUDGET KIT* and *PERSONAL BUDGET PLANNER* are two tools for aiding in the task.

Even single parents who declare they are already on the tightest budget imaginable, still need to go through the process of review and analyze their spending. Indeed, a lack of child support and a very low income may create a nearly impossible situation. Unfortunately, even the hard-pressed single parents often over-indulge in "eating out" or buying "fast food" that costs considerably more than home-prepared meals. Of course, home prepared meals that are ready for the microwave or oven may be little savings. Parents cannot hide behind "I don't have time," because cookbooks with a large variety of thirty-minute meal suggestions are readily available. Spaghetti and macaroni and cheese have always taken less than fifteen minutes to prepare. (Much cheaper than fast food french fries).

No set answers fit all people. It does seem that nearly everyone can benefit immensely by learning how to make and follow a budget. For those who have not learned how to save, a budget is the first step to that process.

Simple Ways To Save Money

There are more ways to save money than by putting a dollar in a savings account. Remember that money does matter: it is a necessity for living today and planning for tomorrow. Take note of these following suggestions.

As for car repair, the advice is be careful about agreeing to repairs or extras that are not needed. Many recent articles have many suggestions on how to avoid getting ripped off. For example, because later model cars have fuel-injection and computerized electronic-ignition systems, spark plugs can last 30,000 miles and spark-plug wires can last 50,000 or more. The general advice is don't get a tuneup unless your car is hard to start, lacks its normal acceleration or has become less fuel efficient.

Average cars still operate better and engines last longer on regular oil changes. It is better to check all hoses. If one is deteriorating, the advice is: replace all. Some types of preventive maintenance save many dollars in the long run. Once you find a mechanic you like and trust, stick with him. Many states or metropolitan areas have emissions tests required before obtaining a license plate every year. A mechanic who is familiar with your car can help you at that time.

Be very careful about having auto repair (or home repair) done without getting at least two estimates. A book editor mentioned saving $500 on one instance of car repair. My persistence when my car broke down while travelling paid off in a similar fashion. I could have waited for a very expensive computer type ignition repair or accept another suggestion.

The alternative suggestion was to blow-dry the computer system which had acquired moisture through an unobserved window leak. It worked and saved a bundle of money.

Perhaps I should explain about the unknown window leak. My front window had been broken and repaired, but because I lived in an almost desert climate it had not really been tested. On a long trip through a different climate my car literally quit running as I drove along in a blinding rainstorm. I considered myself extremely fortunate to have been close to an exit, onto which my car sputtered and exited the interstate. How lucky can you get? A large mechanic-on-duty type of service station was the first thing off the exit!

Men and women should find a mechanic-minded friend, who can befriend them against auto mechanic rip-offs. Betty*, a never-married government employee, thinks she has partially solved the problem. When her car needs work, she tells the mechanic "her husband will be by to check on it," and then has a buddy go by and actually check on the repair. According to various articles women are not the only ones susceptible to illicit auto repair. In this highly technical world there are just as many men as women who are not mechanically-inclined. All need a friend who is!

Some times it is very obvious when specific parts of your car need maintenance or repair. A muffler needs replacing when the noise is obvious, but sometimes other parts of the exhaust system also need replacing. If you have a friend or a mechanic you trust, one of them can get under the car to inspect this. The advice is that if exhaust pipes crush with a pair of pliers, it is time to replace. If they hold up to the pliers and only show a light, rusty powdered coating, then, no. A mechanic should properly advise you even though his shop does not do muffler replacement.

When tires need replacing, consider how long you expect to keep the car. There is a lot of difference in tire cost. Moderately priced tires usually last 40,000 miles, so why buy more expensive tires, if you plan to trade your car in the next year or eighteen months? Depending on the region in which you live, usually one or more tire stores will allow payment without interest in 90 days for the tires you do buy. Plan ahead. Have your tire tread checked and buy tires before an absolute emergency. No need to charge tires on an interest demanding credit card in the event of an emergency. Since the advent of front-wheel drive cars, several of which I have owned, I always have my tires rotated. When I buy tires, I buy two and put them on the front and never buy four tires at a time. Proper tire rotation and balance adds much life to tires, do not forget that.

If second opinions are appropriate in the medical field, why not in the auto mechanical realm? Unfortunately, auto dealer's shops usually have very set prices for every piece of work. If you get an estimate from the dealer, why not get an estimate from other locally owned shops? Better yet, as Betty has discovered, have a someone check it out. Several magazine articles in recent years warn of differences in costs of car repair. Exerting care in purchasing tires, a battery, a muffler, or getting oil changes could easily net an extra $100 a year.

To all singles everywhere: are you sure you need all that television? With the increased cost of basic cable, is all that extra really necessary? For those with a VCR, might it be less expensive to rent a movie now and then than to pay the extra required for HBO? Lowering cable costs by $15 a month, renting two $1.99 movies, nets $11 a month, or $132 a year.

For those who are in job positions requiring very dress up attire, dry cleaning is a monetary concern. Here again, the advice is know your cleaner, patronize places with experienced spotters (Hannon 117-119). Advice comes in the form of plan-ahead. Consider buying clothes you can wash at home. Learn to live without pleats, sequins, or beads. Gradually replacing a wardrobe with garments that can be cared for at home is money in the bank. Replacing one garment that needs to be cleaned at the rate of $5 a week should save $200, if compared to laundering at home. Those of us who have worked on jobs away from home usually know the trick of steam pressing a few wrinkles by hanging a garment in a steamy bathroom. Over-laundering and over-dry cleaning will wear out clothes faster.

If every dollar counts and only one dollar a week is spent on a lottery ticket, that is $52 a year. Find five ways to save $52 and you have $260. Do not be misled by promoters of state lotteries that lottery money will be spent on education. In the event lottery ticket purchasers feel "they are contributing to education," it is not so. California, Florida, Illinois, New York, and West Virginia all spent a smaller percentage of their budgets on education in 1994 than when lotteries were instigated, after publicizing that lotteries would help with education funding (Keating 157-164).

Banking has become more expensive than a few years ago since the deregulation of financial services, according to an industry report in 1996. The banking industry reported record earnings in the three years prior and that was attributed to raised old fees and invented new fees. As many as 100 different kinds of fees now exist in banks. Another trend in banking is the consolidation of banks so that the number has shrunk from 14,000 to about 10,000, with no slowdown in sight (*Consumer Reports*). If bank fees seem to have gotten out of hand, take time to compare bank fees in your area. An article in *Consumer Reports* issues some precautions, such as reviewing your banking records, watching out for "special deals," which may not be all they seem, and not using bank services you can buy elsewhere such as a check supply. The same report revealed that fees can vary as much as $40 a month in any city. The message is clear: it pays to shop, even for a bank. A savings between five and ten dollars a month is worth changing banks.

The great American weakness is probably "eating out," as both "fast food" chains and restaurants abound. If "eating out" has your budget in a bind, it is time to make an adjustment. Many live-alones have solved the problem of "cooking too much," by cooking and dividing portions to be frozen for another day. Every meal eaten at home instead of at a restaurant probably saves three to five dollars per person, depending on the locale. If five dollars is saved a week, there is another $260 for the savings account.

Buying staple groceries on sale is money saved. The same is true with toiletries. Factory outlets and discount chains as well as end of the season sales, offer plenty of opportunities to buy clothing at a savings. Groceries, toiletries and clothing are part of any basic budget, so a savings in any category is money earned.

Add the possible savings in car repair, gambling, dry cleaning, banking, dining out, groceries, clothing, and TV cable. Saving in several of the areas described should net at least $600 a year that could of course, be transferred to a savings account.

According to another article in *Consumer Reports*, $50 a month at only 5% interest will compound and grow to more than $41,000 in thirty years(46-47). What person with no savings today can deny the value of having at least $40,000 thirty years from now? Any new and worthwhile habit has to have a beginning, be it exercising or saving or volunteering. The most important factor is to stop procrastinating. Obviously the idea of $50 a month is to make you stop and think. If you live in an area where the cost of living is high and you intend to retire there, you must plan your savings accordingly. You certainly need to look into a personal retirement savings plan, if you have not.

If you are suddenly serious about saving and investing, take to heart the story of Anne Scheiber, who did not start investing until she retired from the IRS at age 51 in 1943. She took $5,000 from her savings and invested in stocks. She lived fifty more years and willed her money to a university that didn't even know her. Her estate was worth $20 million, and she left it to a nonprofit institution so that the IRS did not receive estate taxes. She avoided a lot of capital gains taxes, because she didn't sell her stock. She understood the value of holding stock through good and bad times, plus the value of investing in already established corporations.

Anne was an attorney who worked for IRS. She had never received a promotion when she retired. Apparently she was angry at the IRS for her treatment and set about to make money and avoid paying taxes on her investment. Because she did not spend her earnings but let them accumulate and then gave them to a non-profit organization she never paid any taxes (Glassman 45-48).

Ms. Scheiber's story is unique, but it also shows what can happen with a plan. Singles need to consider all advice about savings, but especially to begin immediately to "pay yourself first," as discussed in the next section.

Pay Yourself First

No one is suggesting that everyone should save millions of dollars only to leave it to heirs or a school. Do that, if it is your heart's desire. Economists have issued warnings concerning finances in the 21st century that warrant a new resolve for saving money for emergencies and retirement.

"Always pay yourself first" is a philosophy taught by some parents, many sales organizations and some corporations. Parents who practice and teach saving money usually raise children who have learned the importance of saving. Many corporations conduct seminars or workshops, explaining a company savings plan and its benefits. The plans are usually quite flexible, can be increased in amount at given times, and usually have a company or corporation input. If such is not available, the least an individual could do with little effort is to sign for an automatic savings account, a savings bond deduction every month or an Individual Retirement Account (IRA). The computer age creates a substitute for self-discipline by allowing mutual-fund companies and others to take money directly from a bank account every month or quarter.

The idea of being a millionaire seems to have universal appeal, yet 100 million Americans gambled 400 BILLION (39 billion went to the house) in 1997, hoping they would strike it rich (Keating 157-164). While the risk of loss is almost a total certainty in gambling, the risk in a small, consistent investment is almost nonexistent. The majority of the nation's millionaires are self-made; they have not gained their money by inheritance. They are your neighbors, not just someone in Hollywood or New York City.

Arnaud Loustalot (real name) developed his saving habit by watching his mother. His mother made all the family members put their pocket change on the table every day; then she took all the dimes to put away into savings. From that start Loustalot developed the habit of saving ten percent of his salary in stocks, then reinvesting the dividends. Loustalot retired in 1976 from a government job and now has four million in stocks. He said that he is living proof that anybody can become rich (Fitzgerald 32).

If singles can learn and discipline themselves to give a designated amount to their church, they can learn to save for themselves in the same way. Fifty dollars a month is a realistic amount to save, even for most single parents if they are not on welfare. As with any resolve in life, it takes effort and planning. If $50 is really too big for a start, consider a U.S. Savings Bond, available for only $25, which will be worth $50 at maturity. Series H & HH bonds pay a guaranteed rate of four percent. Many banks will deduct a bond from checking or savings every month. Bonds may be a good way to begin to pay yourself. They are not as tempting to use as a savings account with easy withdrawal privileges.

The most important facet of saving is to *DO IT NOW.* Do not procrastinate. Singles often think they will find Miss or Mister Right and that together a retirement plan can be developed. The glaring statistics are a reminder that there continues to be more rather than fewer single people, which means more must plan for their own retirement and emergencies without the aid of a partner. It is true both men and women usually have to make significant adjustments the first year or two alone after a death or divorce. It doesn't take a math whiz to recognize that it costs more to operate two households than one household or one household if there is loss of a spouse's income.

Plans for the future must include everything: new friends, new goals, many adjustments, new budgets, and a positive approach to saving for the future, regardless of how secure or insecure the future seems. However, life does have its rainbows, a few of which will be mentioned in the next chapter.

EIGHT
LIFE'S RAINBOWS

Inspiration, Motivation, - A Reason to Live

Inspiration can bring about motivation, which in turn provides the reason to live. As the suicidal person moans,"I have no reason to live," the widowed mother of four quietly decrees, "I must find a way; my children need me." The reasons for wanting to live in spite of chaos or poverty or death are not always easy to explain. On close observation and analysis, the reasons often seem to center around the desire to do something for someone else or the abiding faith that the situation will get better.

Stories of inspiration and motivation to overcome unlikely odds appear monthly in many national magazines, beginning with the *Reader's Digest* and the countless others on the news stands. Very often the inspiration to perform a good deed or to overcome poverty or to be productive in spite of a physical birth defect has come from a parent.

Dana is my daughter who has lived with a debilitating muscle disease since she was nine years old. Dana is reluctant to consider herself disabled or handicapped, although she clearly is. When her disease was at a low ebb, she was in a vocational school finishing high school requirements. AT&T was recruiting office personnel. Dana passed the screening test, then the test for employment. As she filled out the job application, she clearly wrote the name of her disease as answer to the questions about health problems. Dermatomyositis is not commonly known and she never knew if the information was overlooked or not understood. No one questioned whether the disease might cause problems so Dana worked for the sales and marketing division of AT&T for five years before her health forced her to leave.

To this day, Dana, who is 33 and officially on disability, refuses to give in to her disease and pushes herself to do physical activity, never mentioning to most people that she might be limited. Dana says, "My mother never told me I could not do activities that others did, so I tried everything, including roller skating and ice skating."

Inspirational stories about people who overcame adverse life situations to succeed often motivate others to succeed. Singles who are bored or tired of a job or a location might find inspiration in reading about others who have made changes. If a person desires a change in occupation or in geographic location, help is available. To find out what is available in the projected job market, a community college counselor can help. Counselors can usually furnish reading material and often arrange aptitude tests if a person is considering a different type of work. To learn more about other geographic locations, a travel agency will have free brochures and information can be requested from any state department of tourism for a specific area.

William Rouse warns in "*Best Laid Plans: Discovering Who You Are and Where You Are Headed*" that often company managers and workers in general are so wrapped up in company planning that life plans are neglected. First as Rouse explains, a person needs to discover who he is and find alternative futures that best match his own possibilities. A person can then design paths that will create these futures and commit himself to one of these paths. Singles about to embark on a new life would be wise to take Rouse's advice (34-38).

In many cases, a bereaved or emotionally upset person looks for inspiration and a reason to carry on just to make it through the day at hand. Miniature flip charts with inspirational messages or Bible verses are now available. One in the bathroom or on the kitchen table might provide just the words needed to help start a new day.

The singles who find themselves distressed or in a rut and barely able to accomplish daily chores need to look for inspiration. Inspiration and motivation are like coping skills in that they cannot be purchased in a store or found in a computer program. Perhaps the unmotivated person needs to make a list or plan to do something different, then seek inspiration to carry out the plan, if necessary. In *Coming Back* Ann Kaiser Stearns emphasizes that turning points in life represent a departure from the usual. Ms. Stearns is only one of many authors who recommend activity, not passivity. She suggests recalling individuals and events in the past that can provide strength, hope, and encouragement (315-316). Plans for a different day can include something as simple as a walk in a different direction or a trip to a library or a museum. She also suggests that doing one simple act of kindness for someone else may be a turning point in recovery.

Look at Clouds From Both Sides

The words in the once popular song suggested looking at both sides of the clouds. That may ring an unpleasant chord for all those who expected marriage to last forever. Premature death and unwanted divorce cast many people into a single status they neither expected nor welcome. Those who entered into a marriage they thought would last a lifetime are suddenly seeing the world from a different angle. The bottom of the clouds do not appear the same as the top of the clouds. The single world scarcely resembles the double world.

Anyone who rides an airplane high above the clouds for the first time is probably surprised at the sight of clouds from above. True, clouds have been a fascination of photographers and the object of study of meteorologists for many years. A brochure or an article describing different types of clouds rarely pictures how clouds look from ten or twenty thousand feet above the earth. An awesome adventure is to leave the ground in an airplane when the ground is covered with fog, then to go above the clouds to the sunshine and see the billowy tops of the clouds. They appear soft, yet firm enough for sitting and unbelievable in their beauty. Unfortunately, the side of life without a partner does not usually portray any beauty or inspirational pictures, at least not when it first occurs.

The side of life without a partner can be devastating, especially when all of life seemed to be planned around an ideal of husband, wife and family. When I consented to divorce after thirteen years of marriage in what started to be a dedicated Christian home, the impending differences were shocking. I did not adjust quickly but managed to remain grounded in my Christian teachings. I felt God used the experience of divorce and living alone to teach me so I would stop being so critical of people who are divorced. I never in my wildest imagination thought I would ever divorce, I thought there was absolutely always a way to avoid divorce.

The old Indian adage that "you must walk in another's moccasins" to understand their ways and feelings is true. A slightly different analogy was a favorite story of an Oklahoma evangelist Fred Cherry as he preached against "judging others." Rev. Cherry said that he had been over in Eastern Oklahoma, east of Muskogee at the Arkansas River. It was possible to stand on the big bridge that crossed the river and look at the big, slow river below. The easternmost part of the river at that point was muddy. It was muddy because the smaller Verdigris River had entered just a little way upstream.

The preacher said he could hear the big river talking to the little river and this is what it said. "You sure are muddy and ugly, what is wrong with you?"

The little river replied, "If you had been over the same ground I've been over, you would be dirty, too."

Those who have re-entered the single world may have to work harder, pray longer, dress better and accomplish more in order to portray beauty in the other side of life that the double world is often so quick to criticize. The view and the picture is different on both sides of the clouds, but each can have its own beauty.

Some of us are inspired by others' actions or spoken words or merely by observing the earth and the sky. Another source of inspiration available are the books in the library.

Have You Been to the Library Lately?

Those who have not been to a library in years will encounter a whole new world. Libraries have entered the computer age. By entering a subject on the screen, a list of available books will appear. Library assistants are helpful to direct new users of libraries. They will explain how to use the computer system and other library equipment, such as microfilm readers and copiers. Libraries are the source of a lot of free material, including videos. As far as I know, library cards are available and free to everyone. In times of a financial crunch this is a source of free books, movies and often genealogy services. Take advantage.

Inspiration to reach goals can be found by ingesting daily doses of inspirational thoughts. It is not necessary to purchase inspirational reading material for the library abounds in such. When a person becomes goal-oriented and has a specific field of endeavor in mind, he can read books in that field, which may bolster his enthusiasm.

For fifty years spanning the late nineteenth and early twentieth century, a preacher-lecturer named Russell Conwell told stories about opportunity. His lecture was named "Acres of Diamonds," and it was first published in book form in early 1900. The stories told never seem to grow old. The book is a classic in inspiration. Simply — it contains many stories about people who thought that life would be better in another location, but later discovered "acres of diamonds" in their own back yard. Perhaps the most inspirational side note concerning Conwell, is that he earned about seven million dollars from his lecture tours, and he gave it all away. He gave most of it to help students continue their education. Conwell founded Temple University, originally with the idea that young men could work in the daytime and attend classes in the evening.

Where better to find inspirational role models than in books? Since 1990, publications concerning single parenting, living alone, divorce, grief, change, surviving loss, and family issues have increased. Nearly all the books surveyed have numerous contemporary examples of how others have dealt with these problems. Those unwilling to join in a support group may find answers and inspiration between the covers of books.

Observation: Roses and Rainbows

As Stearns, Bozarth-Campbell, Mandino, and others have emphasized, action is necessary to make healing or any plan a reality. Roses will bloom and days will pass, but the beauty of each will be lost unless each person puts life into a forward mode.

"I lost two years," sighs Robert*, as he explains how he felt about doing nothing, observing nothing, and grieving too long after his wife died. "I really wasted time," he adds, "and I know that now."

Activities will help each one re-awake to life's roses and rainbows. The symbolic nature of a rose has been quoted so often it may seem trite but it is true that life as well as a rose has thorns in addition to beauty.

To those who have an established faith in God and a belief in teachings of the Bible, there is an added inspiration to the beauty of the rainbow. The promises concerning no earth-covering rain may be important, but the beauty of a rainbow seems to serve as a reminder that life can contain beauties as well as spiritual rainfall. God must have known that humans need rainbows. When life is glum and seems hopeless, a sudden rainbow can create unexplained hope.

One summer when I made one of my customary trips to visit my mother who lived in another state, it seemed everything went wrong. I had car problems the whole trip. My mother was not doing well and I hated to leave her alone (mother's choice). A lot of rain while travelling added to my sadness. One evening near sundown as I was returning home, I stopped to visit a cousin in Denver. Suddenly, there it was: a vivid full rainbow. I felt better from having seen it, although nothing about the trip had changed.

Jeff Rennicke wrote about rainbows in *Backpacker* and left a page in his notebook blank, thinking some day he'd find the words to describe how the rainbow affected emotions as well as the appearance of the valley. He realized the rainbow made a gloomy atmosphere disappear and filled the valley and his mind with hope. (67-69)?

Rennicke had been backpacking for six days in rain when the sun's rays met raindrops to form a perfect rainbow in a valley ahead. He said that the rainbow was so bright the spires of the spruce trees below seemed lit like candles and that if light could make sounds it would have sounded like a symphony(68).

Rainbows tend to do that — create feelings of hope and optimism after gloom and fog. Singles especially need rainbows. Singles, especially single parents, also need to find a quiet place.

Find a Quiet Place

Everyone needs a quiet place, but single parents and single executives often carry extra burdens without the support of another person and quiet time should be on the must list. Life in the single lane can be more stressful than the double lane. It is presumptuous to think that stress can be alleviated without special effort.

Stress workshops usually emphasize a time-out-type of strategy in which the individual counts to a certain number, takes deep breaths, closes eyes or otherwise uses some planned method to take a break from the stressful situation. This may be the best strategy while on a job but to carry the idea into home life, everyone needs a quiet place. The location will be as varied as the places in which people live.

A quiet place is not without sound. Only for the deaf is

there no sound, but the sounds created by man are often nerve-wracking, irritating, distracting, and stressful. In order to refresh, regroup and to face the morrow, a quiet time can be invigorating and inspirational. Quiet places can be filled with noises of the earth but without those created by man.

Cynthia is a divorced nurse who lives in the Pacific Northwest. To her the most inspirational quiet place is actually noisy with creatures of the sky and sometimes giant waves crashing on big rocks. The sea gulls are noisy, the eagles are awesome and the waves are sometimes belligerent. Cynthia claims the ocean is the most relaxing place on earth.

While I lived in North Central Washington I sometimes drove to a nearby summit to meditate and marvel at God's wisdom and graciousness. The summit is called Buttermilk Butte and was only a few miles from my home in the very small town of Twisp. The butte is more than 5000 feet in elevation and affords a 360 degree view of the surrounding area. Tall evergreens fill the valleys and tiny lakes can be seen among the trees. It is, indeed, a quiet place.

Sam was a divorced doctor in South Texas. He loved to visit the Gulf Coast and would spend hours walking along the beach in the bay areas. To him, it was the most relaxing quiet he knew. He said, "It is perfect for me."

Those who live in a very rural area are so fortunate, because the countryside is within easy reach. Tiny creeks and dead end roads that used to follow a river, or those that climb high into the hills where a house or two may be hidden, are restful possibilities for quiet places. It is not necessary to be on an ocean shore or on a mountain top to find quiet, but those who learn to find a quiet back yard or a nearby park for refreshment are wise to do so. The mind and body cannot be in constant motion without being replenished of their nutrients. Although the Scripture teaches that it is not good for man to be alone; it likewise teaches to be still and listen (Psalms 46:10a).

Houses built the past half century often omitted the common front porch of the past. In the south it seems the porches are seldom used. Perhaps it depends on the geographic location and whether air conditioning is a part of the life-style. If everything happens in a cycle, as is theorized by some, the front porches will soon be reclaimed as marvelous places for quiet times. Learn how to use quiet times for rebuilding the body and mind which have become weary. Who knows — relax and you may fall in love!

It's OK To Fall In Love

Many are so bitter from the distress of divorce or so saddened by the loss of a mate in death they declare they will never be in love again. As the numbers of those living alone as never-married and single-again continue to rise rapidly, it becomes realistic that many will never experience the situation of being "in love" with another person. Perhaps they can fall in love or develop a passion for a specific cause or activity.

Love is of many colors and many facets. Love goes by many names and includes many activities. Roget's Thesaurus has at least two pages of synonyms and connotations of the word love. Webster's dictionary and Reget's Thesaurus indicate that love is the feeling experienced when one is strongly attached or deeply devoted to another and also a strong liking or deep interest, as in the love of country or love of learning."

This book segment has nothing to do with love and marriage, only about the privilege of falling in love and yes, falling in love can include people, but also inanimate objects and places and the deep satisfaction that can bring.

When I left the southwest and travelled to the far northwest I was fulfilling a life time dream. When I read about the Pacific Northwest and its mountains in geography lessons as I child, I harbored a dream of going there some day. When the opportunity presented itself I seized it. Falling in love again was far from my mind. After a year in Washington state's mid-section, I firmly declared my love for the geography of the area. I could see gold in the hills, the apples, the sunset, the wheat fields, and often commented on my love for the area. I felt that no love from the opposite sex would be necessary for me to enjoy a full life in the years to come.

Cynthia is the nurse who enjoys the noisy ocean as a quiet place, away from frustrations of emergency room nursing. In recent time she has taken photography courses to gain more knowledge and expertise in her second chosen career. Her love for photographing all of the earth's wonders — from exquisite flowers to snow covered mountain peaks has convinced her that falling in love with a person is not necessary for a happy life.

Sam, who loves to walk the beaches of south Texas for quiet, claims his love for plants and flowers is quite fulfilling. His nursery is not only his retirement business, but what he prefers to do with his time. The nursery and its needs are a motivation to live, as much as a family could be.

Examples in "*Happily Never Married*" indicate that most never-married women did not plan it that way, but accept their life-style by the time they are 50, and are truly happily never married (Toufexis 80). The same may be true of heterosexual never-married men, although not much is written on the subject. At some point past 40, those unmarried for any reason seem to have accepted their position and found happiness in some activity or occupation.

Of the never-married singles interviewed for this book, only a few admit to planning *NOT* to marry. Betty planned to spend her life in jobs that would allow her to live in and visit other countries. She maintained close family contact and retired with satisfaction of having fulfilled her own dreams. She lived in several countries and visited many more. Her opportunities to marry were declined but she says now that her life work is complete she would marry the right person, if one happened along.

Most of the singles who took part in the surveys for this book and declare they are very happy now have found a deeper satisfaction in their jobs or the pursuit of some life-long dream. One is Frankie Sue Gilliam, who publishes a regional, historical tabloid *TWIN TERRITORIES.* Frankie Sue has been divorced and widowed but truly loves what she does and makes forceful statements on living alone. She is happy, busy, productive, and says that marriage again would be acceptable, but she is not expecting it. "It would be like the icing on a cake," she says. "The cake is good without it, but like cake, life is good, and a good marriage would be like icing."

Mark has his own business, a florist shop, in Seattle, Washington. Mark likes to ski in the nearby mountains as well as surf in the ocean. His family, which lives in another state, cannot quite understand his lack of desire to marry and have a family. "Maybe, some day," he says, "but I could not be any happier than I am now. It would really have to be someone awfully special to get me to change my life."

Most single people understand their own lifestyle well and think that in a few decades the rest of the world may catch up. In the meantime they will fall in love with whatever and whomever they please.

THE WAY OF LOVE

Take a rosebud and crush it.
Paint a sunrise, but cover it with black clouds.
Describe God's handiwork and destroy the writing.
Mold an exquisite vase and break it.
Take a love, then spurn it, and you will do to a life
what has been done to the rose, the painting, and
all the rest.
Take a rosebud and let it open.
Paint a sunrise, and display it in a frame.
Describe God's handiwork and put it in print.
Mold an exquisite vase and fill it with flowers.
Take a love and receive it, enjoy it, share it, and you
will do for a life all that was done to the rosebud,
the painting, and all the rest.

By Marjorie Barton

NINE
LIFE'S HOLIDAYS AND CELEBRATIONS

BELIEVE - Holidays Need People

From the time of the holy days, as recorded in the Bible and other ancient writings, the days of celebration have included a gathering of people. No record seems to exist of a holy day meant to be spent by one person alone except priests on occasion.

Holy days still exist and are observed by every religious group, but nearly every nation on earth has designed its own special days and the word has become holiday. The most common holidays are declared and observed in all states. As in holy days, holidays are meant to be celebrations. It is difficult to celebrate alone. Several who answered surveys mentioned that New Year's Eve was the worst holiday to spend alone.

Most dictionaries also clarify that a holiday is a day of freedom from labor, a day of rest and recreation. Occasionally, a single person may do well on a minor holiday by resting and doing tasks or taking outings geared for being alone, but on major holidays being with others seems important.

Dr. Joyce Brothers, psychologist and television personality of the late-twentieth century, states that the best method of making holidays easier involves planning. She said the best solution is to surround yourself with people. Another possibility of keeping your mind off yourself, Brothers added, is hard work (*Widowed* 228-230). Many of those living alone have no family close by, but volunteer for tasks such as helping a church serve Thanksgiving dinners to homeless and others less fortunate.

Dr. Brothers' advice is directed to widows but most of the suggestions work well for those alone for any reason. As depression seems to heighten its impact around holidays, those who are mildly depressed need to take precautions and seriously plan for holidays. Dr. Brothers says that you cannot turn holidays and anniversaries into happy occasions, especially the first year, but planning ahead will help the bereaved live through those times more easily (231).

Work is medicine for healing. What better time to lend a helping hand than during holidays? Churches, senior centers, hospitals and sometimes nursing homes have need of special help during holidays. Helping serve meals often has unexpected benefits as those serving feel especially lifted in spirits when they see first-hand the plight of others less fortunate and experience the sincere appreciation of those being served. Helping to serve holiday meals is another avenue of service as well as passing time not only limited to widows and widowers. My single daughters attend a church which serves a Thanksgiving dinner to people who live alone or who have no home. They helped with the dinner last year.

I fall in love often but usually with a geographic location such as the Pacific Northwest. One year I found myself alone on Thanksgiving due to very bad weather in the mountains that canceled a planned trip. Through no fault of friends who thought I had gone on the trip, I was totally alone in my country home. I tried to do other things that interested me but by the time the day was over, I vowed never to spend that holiday alone again. I knew that just going to help serve dinner at one of the churches or senior center in town would have provided the fellowship I had grown to love in my life time. Being with people is often the only requirement for a good time.

A problem not mentioned in most books is the reaction of children to spending holidays away from their extended families. When I spent seven years teaching on the Gulf Coast in south Texas, I was 500 or more miles from other family members. I seldom could arrange to spend any holidays with my parents or other relatives. On one such holiday, my children (all under 13) complained that they were bored. One blurted out, "I hate holidays." I realized that the children noticed other families either had company for the holiday or went to celebrate with someone. I decided to plan all holidays in the future so that the children would experience the attitude of "celebrating" with others.

The holiday that brought forth the comment was the Fourth of July so when Thanksgiving approached, I enlisted my children and others to find people who might be alone. Through friends I found a man and his son who would have to spend Thanksgiving without their extended family. We invited them and two other singles to dinner. Everyone had a grand time. The children agreed that people make holidays special. Being related is not necessary to have a nice time.

Believe the Statistics - Find Someone

Single people who are adjusted to their life-style, be it recent or long-term, may want to consider it a duty to help those less adjusted through holidays. Recognizing that new singles may be in a different stage of recovery and adjustment, it behooves everyone to listen to others who may be sending forth a desperate cry for help. Depression is naturally worse for most during holidays, so it is important to let go of concern for self and help others, if possible.

If a person reading this book has recognized his own depression as suicidal in nature, he should be aware that holidays may magnify his problems and should make plans to spend them with someone who cares. If friends and family are not available, other help is, so CRISIS lines or hospitals can be put to use.

On the other hand some singles find the major holidays, such as Thanksgiving and Christmas tolerable, because they spend it with other family members. No surprise to this author, several survey respondents said that New Year's Eve was the absolute worst holiday. Family get-togethers are common on Christmas with many flying home or making special effort to get to a parent's house. After Christmas or whatever festivities are celebrated the single is left alone to plan for New Year's. If the single doesn't have a date, there seems to be no appropriate place to celebrate New Year's Eve. The programs planned at some churches seem to have little appeal for the average single.

I usually spent Thanksgiving and Christmas with children even after they were grown but the New Year's Eve dilemma was my problem. Although I did not date much, I still liked to be around people, especially on holidays. As one New Year's Eve approached and I did not have a date, I decided to go to the local Eagles' Club. I was still rather new to the area and hadn't had much time to make single friends. I knew there would be singles at the club and hoped I could find some with whom to visit and pass the time. I went and did have a decent time. It was much better than staying home watching the new year arrive on television.

Another answer to the New Year's situation depends a lot on your job. Volunteer to work. Cynthia (the nurse daughter) has told of times when nearly everyone on duty on New Year's Eve would be single. They would plan to party (food) as much as possible in between duties. A hospital is rarely quiet in the Emergency Room but Cynthia says most of the activity from accidents comes after midnight on New Year's Eve. Everyone would bring dips, crackers and cookies and then they would take turns watching fireworks they could see from outside the hospital.

Another possibility for the New Year's Eve dilemma is for the single to do the planning. New Year's Eve would be a good time to show a few friends in the couple world that singles and couples can have a good time together. I know many couples who do not go "out" on New Year's eve, but might welcome a little party in someone's home. Depending on the age group, but if you know some couples with young children who can't afford big parties, let them come and put the little ones to sleep on pallets, while the adults enjoy watching the new year come in. Give that some thought!

Some couples argue over having more women than men. Ask most single women. They don't care if they have a date, they would just like to spend the time in a happy party atmosphere. Here again, the idea of conversation is of utmost importance. New Year's Eve is supposed to be a time to celebrate, not mourn.

Oh, Yes, It's Sad to be Alone

Holidays are not the only types of celebrations that singles often encounter alone. Promotions, awards, and the reaching of long-planned goals create a feeling of celebration. Experiencing an unusual phenomenon like a double rainbow or a moonset on the ocean is more exciting when there is someone with whom to share the experience. Finding a rare fossil or a gemstone while rock hunting, discovering a wild flower that seems different from the rest, and gazing across mountain peaks are other joys to be shared.

While I was teaching in south Texas, I could ususally find someone to go rock hunting or picnicking if I tried. I could also find other children to share the outdoors with my children if I planned ahead.

One day I encountered a problem for which I had no answer. I had been chosen to do a job in the central office of special education. It was job I thought I might like in the future. I had already begun graduate work with that in mind. The position offer came as a surprise. I didn't really expect my children to understand my jubilant feelings and I wished I could think of some way to celebrate. This happened early in the aftermath of divorce. Working, going to school and child-care had taken up so much time I had no close friends in the vicinity.

Some who have lost a mate by death may feel it is appropriate to stay closed in a room on the date of the first important anniversary after the death. Perhaps it is best to be with another family member or a friend who understands the importance of the special day. As writer Alla Bozarth-Campbell explains, not everyone reacts the same to the same circumstances, yet some act very much the same in similar events. She emphasizes that in order to grieve, a person must go through the grief, not around or over, only through it. Anniversaries and holidays must be experienced without the lost mate and each bereaved person must decide his or her strategy (3-5).

The emphasis as always, is to plan, to prepare, to understand that special times will be hard at first. That is why Dr. Brothers and others who have written about grief recommend positive planning to help get through those days (228-230). There are not many recommendations for staying alone during holidays and anniversaries, but singles can certainly make the choice.

Author Philomene Gates insists that if a person is invited to a party, he should go, even if he has to go alone. She says that the times are gone when a hostess has to provide an escort for every woman. She told of her first New Year's party alone when she was so worried about whom she would kiss at the stroke of midnight. She was at a table in an animated, lively discussion when the hostess announced the new year. Everyone made a toast and went back to the conversation (110-113).

Joan Anderson explains that some people are good at the art of celebrating almost everything in life. Some celebrate the end of a work week every Friday night. Others celebrate every child's accomplishment and every anniversary they can recall. She said that if you find someone like this in your circle of friends, you should recognize that person, and take lessons. We all should make every effort to develop our own ability to celebrate life (263).

Ideas for Holidays

All singles do not agree on what to do about holidays, but most do suggest planning ahead. The need to plan ahead for holidays is important for all singles not only those left by death or divorce.

When I moved to Washington state and was in business there, I had little time at first to develop a social life. Winter holidays in North Central Washington were usually well wrapped in snow, but planning ahead allowed me to spend them with others. One Christmas I invited a childless couple from a nearby town to spend Christmas with me. The couple had no family close by so the time together helped everyone.

Dr. Brothers said that she invited 18 people to her farm to spend the first Thanksgiving after her husband's death. She said there were a few tears, but basically she was too busy to think of herself, and the time flew by in a whirl. Couples may enjoy a cruise or travel away from families during holidays, but Brothers does not recommend it for widows. A trip for the prime purpose of shopping or particular sight-seeing may be enjoyable in a year or two, but widowed singles should avoid planned trips where the couple events are so obvious (229-231).

There may be exceptions to these statements as the list of singles grows and grows. One radio station in the northwest sponsors events for singles such as a cruise for singles on an area lake to see all the holiday lights. Dr. Brothers categorizes weekends with holidays. She says they are bad because there are so many of them. She also indicated that she planned weekends a month in advance, so a Friday night would not creep up and remind her that she had nothing to do for the next two days.

My children's father rarely picked them up for the weekend, although it was his privilege to do so. On one summer Friday evening he had taken the children and I could think of nothing to do. I said it was annoying to be so alone and although I could have cleaned house thoroughly, I felt miserable in not knowing what to do. "Working all week, child care and chores every night— that's all right, but Friday night is the pits, when you are alone," I proclaimed.

Respondents to the surveys and writers such as Dr. Brothers say it matters not who you are, weekends and holidays are no fun alone. Acquiring degrees and being a professional does not make it any easier on holidays and weekends than if you are a store clerk or a mechanic or retired. I made comments to my mother about Friday nights and until she became a widow and experienced it, she thought I was a little silly. During a visit after my father died she said then she understood about Friday and weekends.

An idea from Gates' book will work for any Friday or any holiday. Make a list of all — absolutely all the single people you know. Set a date (or a holiday). Call and ask each one if they have a date that day. If they are dateless, invite them to a party. In other words have a party and disallow dates and see what happens. Some are never going to anything that resembles a "singles club", but they may come to a party because of the friendship. If those invited start insisting on knowing who will be there, just explain they are all "your friends," and if they don't want to come, just say so...no offense! (113)

The important issue as a single person is to plan a social life, just as a career and household duties are planned. As a career in any field will not come about without some planning, nor will a financial plan, nor the doing of household chores, why should anyone expect a social life to just happen? Dienstag (a magazine columnist), Gates (author), Brothers (psychologist-author) and others all agree that single people need to be aggressive and make plans for the inevitable holidays and weekends. Planning does not always mean a party, but having a plan and anticipating its realization is usually important to peace of mind and an enriched life-style.

In addition to ideas suggested in the section about holidays, Gates had other ideas. She suggested giving a brunch on New Year's Day; or having a back yard cookout on Labor Day, Either of those ideas might please children, especially if they are not yet in a social circle of their own. New Year's usually signals returning to school and Labor Day is often after school begins.

All holidays have higher traffic accident rates so why not plan to stay home but make it special? I see nothing wrong with inviting friends to share in a pot-luck type of dinner or picnic. That way no one has a big expense. Holidays aren't the only times for fun and singles need to consider other types of outings as discussed in the next chapter.

TEN
LIFE'S OUTINGS

Outings - brief and spontaneous!

Outings can be for the afternoon, the weekend or the summer, which of course depends on your work schedule, retirement plans or your financial ability. Do not disregard the afternoon outings as insignificant. An e-mail just arrived on my computer which reads, "Krystal and I are going to take the girls to the Burger King so they can wear themselves out playing (in the play yard) then they will sleep while we plant flowers and mow the yard. Love, Dana."

Those two single daughters have been attending classes to hone their parenting skills and have learned some good and inexpensive ways to entertain their daughters. What they are doing is very sensible. If the season is appropriate they use nearby parks. For me a simple outing a few miles away to the nearest river bank or coastal beach where I can walk and pick up rocks or shells is living life with interest and refreshment!

No one likes to travel any more than I do. Travelling alone has brought raised eyebrows, verbal questions of sanity and sharp criticism to many singles who by choice or fate travel alone. Travelling alone or with a companion must be a personal choice. I never minded travelling alone and was never afraid. It is simply very obvious that solo travellers need to use good sense.

"Our World," a column in *New Choices* tells it well. One 59 year old woman says she has the same conversation every time she pulls her RV into a campground. The first thing she is asked is, "Are you by yourself?" to which she replies, "No, I've got my dog." Next, it's "Aren't you afraid?"

to which she says, "Of what?" The woman, Arlene Van Note added that at a time when children are grown and you have a list of things you always wanted to do, women often scare themselves out of doing those things (9).

I encountered many such questions as Van Note did, only I was tent camping. Tent camping is less expensive. Many two-man tents are very easy to erect and cost about $20. On one such outing with a gem and mineral club in Washington state, another couple from the club in an RV said they watched with amazement as I erected the tent quickly next to their RV site. They admitted they started to get out and help but decided to watch until I needed help as I seemed so sure of myself. Why not? It was easy!

Another time I decided to spend the night in a Forest Service campground in the North Cascades National Park. Near neighbors watched and said, "If you need anything, just holler!" Campers are friendly 99 percent of the time and helpful, too. I encountered the friendly attitude every time I camped alone — friendly, not aggressive.

Should you be afraid? If you are afraid of living, yes. Crime and violence can be found in cities and villages, in the country and in fast food restaurants. No place is totally safe from the ravages of sick-minded people. Statistically, campgrounds are probably as safe as any other place. It does not hurt to be cautious however, and those camping alone might want to keep a crowbar or some other weapon handy by the sleeping bag. All campers should learn to become aware of all normal safety precautions, such as: never leave food out, not even in a tent. Bears have a good sense of smell!

Unfortunately, vandalism is on the rise so do not leave items such as camp stoves on the table if you are going far from the campsite. Never leave your car unlocked even if you are just taking a short walk.

Several books on inexpensive camping (Less than $10, Less than $5) are available. Triple A has regional RV and Tent Campground directories for members. The US Army Corps of Engineers has Regional Recreation Brochures.

Check with their nearest district office for information on how to obtain pamphlets and maps. Camping is available at a reduced rate for those with a Golden Age Passport (available at 62 and honored in all national parks and other national recreation spots such as Corps of Engineers facilities). Surprisingly, many campgrounds in the nation are absolutely free, usually in remote locations along rivers or in forests and on mountains or desert-like surroundings.

Many others charge only five dollars or less ($2.50 for seniors). You may have to pick up information on a local basis. The United States Forest Service (USFS) and the Bureau of Land Management (BLM) both maintain hundreds of low cost campgrounds.

The United States is so rich in opportunity for simple, inexpensive travel there is little excuse for most people to say they cannot afford to go anywhere. For those city singles who are accustomed to travel by bus, subway, air, and rail, many groups provide opportunities for short and long trips. Check with a travel agent for interesting tours (And the Singles Center via computer on-line).

As in all of life, planning is a must. The first and easiest place to begin to collect travel information is the local Chamber of Commerce. Most would be amazed at the day trips that can be made from any one point, anywhere in the United States. If children are still in the home, remember that they learn the most by active participation and that includes everything from geography to computer games.

Many singles are confronted with whether to go every time they are invited to what seems to be mostly a family affair. Singles should learn to take all such invitations as a viable opportunity of promoting better relations between single and married people.

How to be the Life of a Company Party

As a member of a school faculty of which 80 percent were married, I never liked to go to annual faculty Christmas parties. The principal challenged me one year, wanting to know why I never attended. I explained that nearly everyone brought a spouse and I felt out of place. With his encouragement, I decided to go and made sure that I participated in games and conversation. It was quite an effort that first time but well worth it. I couldn't remember when I had so much fun.

I also had drifted into the habit of staying at home instead of attempting to socialize. After five years as a single parent, I suddenly realized that I no longer had adult conversations. I taught children under twelve, came home and dealt with more children. After the Christmas party, I vowed to be more social because I felt that my children needed to understand that I had a need to socialize the same as they did.

When it is time for the annual picnic or the retirement party, the invitations always seem to emphasize "bring your spouse or date". Many a single person has stayed away from those affairs because they did not have a spouse or date. For many it is difficult to go alone. The advice of Collin Perry is: go anyway. Go and have fun (126). If other single people work at your place of the business, ask them if they are going. If any are reluctant for the same reason you are, challenge them. Say, "I promise I will go, if you will."

A government employee, Rachel*, has also noticed that there are more single women than men in her circle of friends. She is not invited to some social events, because the host attempts to have an equal number of single men and women. A chemistry teacher who also mentioned not being invited, indicated that socializing on weekends would be nice even if everyone else is married. Sometimes the couple world is more concerned with matching their guests than being assured everyone has a good time.

In a column called "Good Manners" a question on this topic seems appropriately answered. A couple planning a holiday party had a guest list of 25 women and 15 men. The wife did not want to have the party on New Year's Eve, because she thought the women would want to be paired off that night. The answer in the column insisted that the couple should invite all their friends to help them celebrate the dawning of a new year—with all its potential for happiness, personal growth and good health (12).

In the orchard country of Washington state, proof of social possibilities is demonstrated by one family that hosts a summer picnic and invites people because they are friends, not because they are couples. The same is true in a reverse situation in Seattle. My daughter Cynthia loves to entertain. She usually has a Christmas open house at which time she invites all her single friends as well as the couples she knows. They all have a good time.

Dr. Joyce Brothers and Roberta Meyer both suggest starting new traditions after becoming single again. Planning events that will include some couples is a subtle way of educating couples to the possibilities of socializing with single people. Some of them admit that they feel threatened or awkward in the presence of single people (228, 161).

All parties could include both singles and couples if the hosts and hostesses would adopt the right attitude. Socializing is a time for sharing ideas, laughing, enjoying other people. Parties should be parties and if singles meet and want to be better acquainted, they can date. Parties do not have to be mating affairs. People should learn to party together because of common interests. Other places where people congregate but not in a social fashion may be awkward for some singles; such as church.

One in the Pew

Do you hate to go to church because you have to sit by yourself and you used to sit with your husband or wife? Try to remember the reason for going to church which was not to show the world your marital status. Now if you are single-again or never-married and decide to start attending church, try not to feel uncomfortable. Perhaps the simplest manner of overcoming the problem is to look for another person sitting alone and ask if you can join him or her.

Attending church alone after having attended as a family unit is often extremely traumatic for the single person. Attending church as a never-married single person also has its drawbacks as most churches make positive statements about marriage and the family but neglect to acknowledge singledom as an appropriate alternative.

Sadly there are true stories about "discrimination" in churches. There are also positive, encouraging, non-discrimination stories. A positive thought includes the fact that the Baptist General Convention of Oklahoma appointed a full-time minister to single adults to begin duties in May, 1997 (Baptist Messenger State paper). This may seem a little late, considering the fact the single adult population has been steadily growing for at least 25 years. It is certainly a step in the right direction.

An article appeared in the "*Forum*" newspaper of Fargo, N.D., in 1997 concerning the large single population in the Dakotas. A retired minister of a United Methodist church in Sioux Falls, N.D., said "We have identified singles as a particular area of need in the church, but have done little in finding long term answers."

According to that newspaper article the Dakotas, Nebraska, Colorado and New York have the highest percentage of people living alone. According to census figures all those states have over twenty-five percent of their *ADULTS* living alone as compared to the national average of about sixteen percent. (About ten percent of the total population live alone.)

More and more churches are recognizing the needs of single adults as being special, such as offering workshops on divorce recovery, grief, and parenting skills. Although churches are not primarily social, the end result of going to church provides opportunities for activities outside the home.

The PTA Meeting, the School Open House

A single parent should consider school functions important and never consider staying away because of marital status. It is very important that you support your child's learning process. Children are not sitting in a judgement seat in the manner of many adults. They are proud to introduce their mother or father to their teachers and doing so adds to their self-esteem. Many married couples have only one parent able to attend school functions for various reasons. One may do shift work (at hospital, factory, etc.); one may have to baby-sit a much younger sibling or one who is sick. There are countless reasons why only one parent may attend. Thus the single parent should not feel out of place at school functions.

Attending school functions, PTA groups, student performances or open houses are also other ways of net-working for single parents. It is a realistic method of meeting other singles or at least learning that single parenting is not a rarity. Although school functions are not thought of as opportunities for socializing in a party fashion, there is much proof that the on-going support of children in school activities lessens the probability of problems children may have in academic setting. Single parents need to make involvement with school a high priority, regardless of their busy schedules.

Why Singles Frequent Bars

Why singles frequent bars may not be the slightest issue in densely populated cities of the United States. About 60 million people live in rural areas and people in those small communities tend to be more critical of others who frequent bars. There it may become an issue. This discussion is for the benefit of those who have failed to comprehend why many singles frequent bars.

Myriads of facts and philosophies are imposed on those who attend college and take even one psychology course. Among those facts are the studies which prove that the basics of human needs are food, clothing, and shelter (Maslov's theory). Co-existence with other humans is the norm. Existence with other humans has always necessitated a form of communication. Clans, tribes, or whatever you choose to call any specific group of people, have always interacted with all of their own group members. That means they have communicated by whatever form was appropriate.

Having established by all norms that communicating with others is necessary and helpful, how then is there such a lack of communication among people when someone is widowed, divorced, or never-married? The single left after a spousal death or divorce seems to have the most difficult time finding people with whom he or she can share his or her feelings of grief, loneliness, and confusion. As job transfers cause a lot of movement in the U.S., so a divorce or death may happen when the person is miles away from old friends and family members. The single may have new acquaintances but no one available as the special support needed at that time.

The problems with communication after becoming single again happen to both men and women. Testimonies of several widowers and divorced men indicate that they rarely went to a "bar" before they became single again. Wayne*, a widower in South Texas, found that he was going to the bar every day after work. He never dated anyone he met there. He did find people with whom to visit. After he met others in a newly formed singles club, someone asked him why he went to the bar. He did not hesitate to say, "I just need someone to talk to after work."

John* was a divorced farmer whose wife left the area, while he remained to farm.

After a day's work he hated to go to the empty house so he chose a bar instead. In the bar people were laughing and talking, and he found someone to share stories, problems, and dreams. The bar scene became the means to end a lonely hour of the day. It was not an intention of John to "get drunk", merely to have some company.

Charlene* was a Christian single who was devastated by her divorce and considered herself a failure. Other singles on her job encouraged her to go with them to a lounge after work and assured her she did not have to drink alcohol. Again the purpose was to have fun and conversation before going alone to an empty house or apartment. Charlene was soon in the habit of going with her colleagues.

At first Charlene could justify her actions because she and several of her friends drank soda, not alcohol, which was an important issue with her. Then Charlene learned that not everyone in a bar gets drunk, which had been her impression growing up in a strict Christian atmosphere. She realized that she was looking for conversation and support. She found that and new friends who helped her understand that divorce is sometimes the only option and she became less critical of herself.

Nothing in advice columns to singles or in books suggesting ways of overcoming loss hints that people should go to bars or lounges to establish new relationships or to explore avenues of communication. Supposedly the fear of promoting alcoholism keeps some writers from suggesting it as an alternative when no support group seems handy. It remains a fact however, that some have thought of no other method to combat their loneliness, except to "go to a bar."

Perhaps the those who want to promote a "Christian Singles Scene" can take note from this and conjure a substitute for "going to a bar." When I had been single a few years, I declared that if I were wealthy I would establish Single Centers that would invite singles to drop by and visit — no purchase required — with free coffee and soft drinks. It's too bad some churches don't latch on to the idea instead of criticizing singles for "going to the bar."

Persons of widely varied backgrounds have made frequent comments in the surveys I circulated about "the bar scene" and "I wish I had found a support group." Others commented that the after work bar scene was a place to vent feelings with friends who don't try to advise or criticize and that it is a type of support group.

Social Opportunities - Make Your Own

Eleanor Foa Dienstag says in "Living Alone" (a column in *New Choices* magazine) that in order to have a successful single life it is important to nurture as vast a network as possible. Dienstag, as well as other writers, has admitted that social planning was a major part of her marriage and that her social life no longer hinged on the same group after becoming single.

Dienstag adds that your social life will flower only if you make it happen. Some of the means of recovering from loss and divorce are being friendly, being interested, being helpful, and being willing to take advantage of available opportunities (Mar '97).

Networking is recent terminology for "making connections." The more places a person goes, the more events he or she attends, the more he or she is likely to have an active social life. Going to church, special interest clubs, political rallies, veterans' organizations, volunteer groups, school support groups, community action groups, all lend themselves to meeting people. You can go forward and actively reinvest in living, as Ann Stearns says in *Coming Back* (315-316).

Indeed, life has many sides: mental, physical, spiritual, and social. Everyone needs to develop the mind, to maintain the physical, to practice a religious faith, and to mingle with others in order to have a balanced existence.

Here is a party idea promoted by some. If you are a woman, invite a lot of single women friends and require that each one bring a male friend (not a lover). Single men can plan a gathering by the same method. The new mix of people can result in new friendships and often new romance. Any variation of the idea can work. The idea is for single people to bring single people, but not all the same sex so that there can be a lot of introductions that might have been difficult to arrange on a one to one basis. Ask anyone who has tried — blind dates are not often a very good idea.

Too many social opportunities are available for anyone to lament they have nothing to do. In the event a person lives in an extremely small community or in the country, there are many other singles in every locale. If a person knows none, then it is time to do a serious search and maybe rescue others from the same lack of knowledge.

Have fun! Live a little! Next we will confront issues of single parenting.

ELEVEN
LIFE FOR SINGLE PARENTS

It Takes Planning, Etc.

It takes a lot of planning to find a balance in life for single parents. Single parents have it all: a missing parent, budget problems, all the emotions, double duty — but rewards of watching their children grow if they can find time. To say single parents are accepted as a norm is not true; to say single parents are praised in all realms of life is not true; to say single parents have a chance to prove statistics wrong is true.

In *Parents* magazine, Christy Scattarella of Portland, OR., wrote of her experience with non-acceptance. She attended a meeting held to recruit mentors for young girls in low-income, single parent homes. Because she was a single mother with a successful career, she decided to volunteer. A recruiter blatantly told her that she didn't think a single parent was a proper role model for a girl in a single-parent household (232).

As Christy wrote that although the purpose of the organization was to bolster self-esteem, its leader refused to expose a young girl to the idea that her own family structure might have merit (232). People are single for many reasons; it is unfair to lump all single parents in the same category as if they are unworthy and incompetent.

Single parents by chance or choice have the same emotional problems and discipline problems that couples have with their children. The difference is that too often they have to solve the problems on their own without consulting a mate. Singles, who chose to be single parents, know that some day they will have to answer a lot of questions, if they chose to have a child out of marriage. In the meantime, this choice of parenting is in the minority. There are about twelve million men and women who are single parents to children, whose problems are and always will be unique in the double world. Most of those single parents have been married.

Several new books on the subject of single parenting would have been very welcome twenty or thirty years ago. Rae Lindsay and Philomene Gates both wrote about widowhood (which happened 20 years go). They seemed to find no handy guides for single parenting at that time. *In Praise of Single Parents* by Shoshana Alexander and *The Single Mother's Book* by Joan Anderson are now in libraries. Surely every single parent would want to use one or both of these new books as a guide to daily living. Even those singles who are single parents by choice seem to agree that raising children alone is less of a deliberate choice than a response to circumstances. All stories in books and articles indicate that single parents face many unexpected problems and sorely need guidance.

Even with the help of good guide books, support groups, church associations, neighbors, relatives and friends, the single parent is still facing media attack, statistics, and subtle discrimination that remind them they are living single when double is more acceptable. Scatterella's story occurred in 1996, not ten or twenty or thirty years ago.

So how are single parents going to raise responsible, well-adjusted, productive adults in an age of dramatic technological change, unsettling crime rates, and not-too-subtle criticism? *In Praise of Single Parents* may have many answers to those questions. Shoshana Alexander says that single parents can waste time focusing on what has been lost or they can turn and embrace what is ahead. They can also stop seeing themselves as victims and begin to create a new life (Chapter 2).

Becoming a single parent may have happened so fast there was no time for planning, but once it has happened, the single parent must take time to plan if he or she is to survive. *The Single Mother's Book* is an excellent, detailed guide book by Joan Anderson. A review of its contents reveals that single fathers and of course, single grandparents who have children to raise, could profit from most of the book. Perhaps because men still tend to earn more than women and because there are fewer single fathers, this book has been directed to women only. (The book did result from a Single Mother's Group, which worked to identify and solve problems of single mothers.) Alexander's book includes all single parents, but is not as specific or detailed in its guidelines — as in day care facilities, finance, court, etc.

Anderson says that with careful planning and the passage of time, your life can and probably will settle down. Anderson is very technical in everything from income tax benefits to how to do common house repairs. She also includes specific lists in sidebars for making goals, changing jobs, locating child-care, dealing with ex-partners (and his relatives) and many other categories of single parenting.

Ms. Anderson's book is meant to be a guidebook for problem-solving similar to some of this book, but focused for single moms. One subject not discussed in this book so far is discipline of children. If discipline is a problem with a very young child, stop and read the next sentence carefully. If a parent has no control at the age of three, what will it be like at thirteen? It is already time to seek help and guidance, such as books, parenting classes or other type of support. Every locale has different options for day care, parenting classes, financial aid, and do not forget government services. Consult the local telephone directory under the name of your state in order to locate a number for various services which may be available. The local Y.M.C.A. or Y.W.C.A may offer workshops or services which would help a single parent. A CRISIS line is usually listed in both yellow and white pages. Look under Human Services in the yellow pages.

Some churches offer a "Parent's Day Out," where children can be left while the parent shops or does other activities. It is not a "day-care" center and the service is usually once a week. Churches in some areas also offer a parent's night out where parents take turns with the child care duties. This is not necessarily limited to a two-parent family. Single parents should not try to be martyrs, doing everything without help. Any time away from children and work can be revitalizing.

Learn to use available services in addition to the better known government agencies for aid to dependent children and food stamps. Government agencies have taken a more active role in attempting to stop child abuse and domestic violence by offering counseling in anger management and parenting. Some classes are designed especially for single parents.

Another idea for planning is to have a regular weekly "family meeting" as soon as the children are old enough to have a discussion. If a child is in kindergarten, he is old enough. Obviously, the older the children, the more it can be like a real business meeting. Anderson suggests doing this on a regular basis. As children sense without being told that life with one parent is not the same as with two parents, a planning meeting can be beneficial in several ways. Children need to understand their role in problems, as well as their role in future plans. They are more apt to work out a solution to a problem if they play a role in discussing it. Children need to be children but they also need to learn to accept responsibility for their actions and household duties. What better way to keep communication lines open than to have weekly family meetings (89-92)?

Some suggestions for what to include in a family meeting are: bath rules, when Mom is not at home rules, weekend plans, changes in household chores, homework rules. If children are teenagers when the parent becomes a single parent, immediate start up of family meetings might avoid unpleasant disagreements and misunderstandings later. Obviously, dating rules, houseguests, and other teenage concerns would be included in family meetings.

Single parents who learn the art of planning ahead in all aspects of their lives might be able to avoid many of the pitfalls and problems which abound nationwide. "I didn't know," is no longer an excuse. Most single parents *ARE* made aware, through countless agencies and/or all media, the problems of drugs, alcohol, teen pregnancy, and sexually transmitted diseases. Add this book to the wake-up call and begin now to plan and act upon your plans immediately.

Time For Fun

When is it time for fun? Busy single parents often have to balance too many chores and already feel too robbed of their own social life to consider having fun with their children. While I taught in south Texas I helped in a community-based singles group that planned outings with children once a month. That type of fun helped my children understand they were not alone in the one-parent world. I also made friends who had children and we often planned smaller two-family outings.

One of my own rules of singledom included singing while in the car. I told the children that they could not change their life just then and they might as well practice being happy. As they were all quite musical, singing was a good thing to do when travel was necessary. We learned a lot of happy songs and singing was fun for us.

Anderson's book contains ideas for "free and cheap fun" to be found in the Nashville area. Most of the ideas are available everywhere in the U.S. One idea not mentioned in the earlier chapter of this book is making use of junk stores, flea markets and yard sales. Most children of the nineties enjoy those outings as much as adults. Give each whatever money the budget will allow and have fun.

A purposeful walk, especially in a rural area, can yield acorns, moss, and various weeds and tree products suitable for use in arts and crafts. Many dried weeds can be spray painted and used in wreaths and other ornamental displays. A hike or walk such as this has many rewards in addition to exercise and togetherness to be experienced by a family. A single parent family should not be devoid of fun just because it operates on a tighter budget. Children usually learn to appreciate inexpensive outings when they are given the opportunity to do so.

When my children were a little older, it became more difficult to plan family outings, but the summer before the oldest was a senior in high school, I insisted. I told my son that he had to arrange his schedule at the pool, where he was a life guard, so we could go camping together for at least four days. The middle and oldest children complained but reluctantly complied. The campout included a float experience on the Guadalupe River. Although it was in the summer and the river was not swift, the trip proved to be such fun that all three complained about "having to go home."

Parents are still parents and often need to insist that the children be included on outings away from home. My experiences proved many times that everyone could have fun and fun is like laughter. Fun provides good memories and is healthy in all aspects. All of my children grew up with a strong appreciation of the outdoors and a firm belief that one needn't pay a fortune to have fun.

Every part of the United States is rich in history, and history is usually only boring when a teacher requires that facts be memorized. It doesn't matter where a person lives; there are back roads and small towns with unique characteristics to be explored. Every single parent can consult the local visitor center or Chamber of Commerce for local brochures for planning day trips that will only require money for gas and a picnic.

Children will be a lot more interested in their own state history if they have visited many points of interest. Why wouldn't children enjoy putting their heads in the stocks at the Ft. Gibson, Oklahoma, fort for a snapshot? Why wouldn't they like to ride through the mountains on an old train such as the one at Eureka Springs, Arkansas, or Durango, Colorado? Why wouldn't they like to see Daniel Boone's grave in the cemetery in Frankfort, Kentucky?

Everyone lives near many points of interest. I wrote a column in my newspaper about exploring the Big Bend of the Columbia River in Washington state, an area which was new and interesting to me. I received lots of mail and comments from readers who said, "Oh, I had forgotten all about that. You reminded me how interesting it is."

Children may be interested in exploration while they are young, such as rattling a piece of bright wrapping paper or banging on pots and pans. Sometimes as they become older they have to be shown that there are interesting things to do beside watch TV or play computer games.

One year when I taught in the west Texas town of Bowie, one of my students learned of my interest in rocks. She said if I could come to her place on a Saturday she would show me petrified wood and fossils. With directions and children in tow I went to the student's home and my, what fun! We found a creek, an out-of-sight canyon, big chunks of petrified wood and fossilized rock. My friends in town said they had no idea there was such a pretty place nearby. It was only five miles from town. Fun is just around the bend; just a little planning away. Life is meant to be fun.

Start New Traditions

Philomene Gates and Shonshana Anderson strongly advocate starting new traditions when a family becomes a single parent family. Nothing is the same in the new family so there is no reason to cling to old traditions, especially when they may contain more hurt than good. Anything that the missing parent did not particularly like to do can be added to a list of "can do ideas". For instance if you want to invite a foreign exchange student for Thanksgiving dinner, do it. If you want to order pizza every Friday night and just relax, do it.

Traditions of honoring children for special achievements

can be developed within each family: a special place at the table, a homemade banner, a special song to be sung by the rest of the family. Children should be recognized but not necessarily rewarded for academic improvement as well as accomplishment for sports and arts achievement and for good citizenship. Some families use calendars with stickers to note achievements. The main thing is that children learn to enjoy learning for the sake of it, not for the reward.

Another tradition being promoted nationwide and individually in homes is the attitude of volunteering. The idea of doing something for someone else is not new, but has received much attention in recent years by such events as "Make a Difference Day" (*USA WEEKEND*). That special day was started in the 90s by the Sunday news magazine to be held on the last Saturday of October. Children in single parent families may be the recipients of other's good deeds, but likewise, they can learn to do kind things. For example, according to the climate and needs of the community, every child can help gather food for food banks or mittens and caps for needy children or items for babies.

Recycling aluminum, glass, and paper may be mandatory in some areas but not in all by far. Recycling is so simple and can bring spending money into the pockets of children in single parent families. Recycling can be a family project or an individual one, but most communities have a recycling center to which to take the items. Recycling can put money in the purse while teaching about the needs of conservation, which brings us to a closer look at finances and single parents.

Money and Single Parents

As a single parent in the 1990s, Georgia* realized as time went by that she was failing desperately in one area of parenting. She was finding it impossible to save money and she knew that she was not teaching her children how to save. After all, if she couldn't do it, how could she teach them?

As it has been established by statistics that single parents have a lower standard of living (financially) than two-parent families, it is obviously more difficult for single parents to consider saving. Most single parents live on the false dream that "it will get better," then "I'll save a little for emergencies." One emergency after another seems to move those plans farther into the future.

In *MONEY DOESN'T GROW ON TREES*, Godfrey and Edwards state that the proof of financial ignorance or illiteracy, as it is called, is in the rising level of personal bankruptcy and a nearly incomprehensible national debt. The authors insist that education is the answer to the financial dilemma and that it must start with children. They also remind that it is as important to learn to spend wisely as it is to save (86-87).

As money is saved for three reasons—for an emergency, retirement, or to make a purchase—it is suggested that younger children be encouraged to save for something they really want. Single parents who have been unable to save can develop plans for themselves and the children at the same time. It is time for both to learn. Chapter five in this book has suggestions for adjusting spending. When parents adjust spending, both they and the children can learn about saving.

After children learn about saving for an object, they can learn about saving so that the savings will grow. It is never too early or too late to start saving.

Godfrey and Edwards provide simple games and instructions for teaching children about money, when to start allowances, how to guide teenagers financially, and how to teach about charities (99-104). Single parents must look ahead into the 21st century, admit the probabilities of the nation's finances and add to their duties an obligation to teach their children that indeed, "money does not grow on trees."

Ex-Partners Can Be Friends

Ex-partners who are parents of children need to set their differences aside and attempt to be friends. It is not wrong to like the other parent for his or her good qualities, even though marriage did not work. It is certainly OK for single parents friends.

All the reasons for divorce and separation, the rights or wrongs, the "what if's?" that cannot be corrected, do concern the children, usually with a negative impact. Whether the ex-partner remarries or lives with someone else or has moved far away does not remove the fact of parenthood. Unless the absent parent refuses to cooperate, efforts should be made to establish a healthy relationship with children. Some states require parenting plans to be filed in divorce situations or in the event there was no marriage and the noncustodial parent wants visitation privileges. If visitation rights can be worked out agreeably and a friendly relationship is maintained, the children will usually benefit. Then the missing parent is usually more cooperative during emergencies. It certainly makes good sense to support your ex-partner's image in the children's eyes (assuming it is worthy) so that they will be proud of him or her. Being proud of the absent parent should also help the children have better self-images. Fathers who have had a good relationship with children by an ex-partner are more likely to be involved in a child's college education when the time comes.

Hopefully, more single mothers will realize the impact and long-range effects of father-child relationships, and will be willing to make efforts to see that those relationships are established or maintained. Children can re-establish a relationship with a parent even though there is a time gap. Letters and phone calls often bridge the gap quickly.

No one has all the answers to single parenting, but research has provided a lot of answers to problems brought on by the absence of a parent. The present generation has a chance to correct the problems of the past by actively attempting to maintain or establish healthy relationships with both parents.

SIPS - Sudden Instant Parent Syndrome

Stories have been written about persons who have married a widow or widower and became instant parents, but this creates a two-parent family. A story could also be told about the single or never-married (usually woman), who never had children of her own and suddenly by choice or circumstance, becomes an instant parent to children not her own.

That happened to Samantha* when she was 40 and her sister and brother-in-law were having such domestic problems they could not care for their two daughters. Samantha had always wanted children but was caught in the "happily never-married" category.

"As suddenly as a tornado," she said, "I was a parent. I was not prepared to be a 24 hour parent. Where does all the time go? Day care, counseling, school, church, shopping, working full time...how do single parents do this?"

Samantha was a born organizer so after she took a deep breath, she knew she had to get organized and "make rules." As is typical of children caught in a whirl of domestic problems, rules had not been part of their lives. The children had lot to learn. First they had been used to very irregular bedtimes; next they rarely ate at the table; and understandably, they were used to getting their way by whining.

Samantha's job and day care coincided fairly well. The children already knew and loved their aunt but structure and discipline were something they had to get used to. Samantha quickly arranged a room for them with beds donated by friends, then set about to help them understand the rules. The children were six and eight and had no comprehension problems, just a history of little discipline.

All meals would be at the table and a fruit snack would be provided by the sitter when the girls first arrived from school. Samantha had to adjust with the rules as she usually had her meal at her coffee table in the living room. Snacking was eliminated from their life almost completely. Table manners were learned, because as Aunt Samantha said, "We have to practice so we can eat out sometimes."

Bedtime was 8 p.m., not 8:30 or 9, which meant that preparations had to begin forty-five minutes before. As they lived in a mild climate, baths were every other night during the school year. The girls took turns choosing the story to be read at bedtime except at least once a week, the aunt read from *The Book of Virtues* or *Winnie the Pooh.*

Rules for Saturday included proper instructions for not waking Aunt Samantha until 8:30 at least. The girls learned when to be quiet and use of the TV was made clear. Progress was made in every category and when the girls returned to their own home six months later, they had learned a lot of lessons that made for harmony.

Samantha said that she would never ever again wonder why single parents had such a hard time. "Your life is not your own any more. It all revolves around the children. It is rewarding, in giving and receiving love, but never let it be said that it could be easy."

Some have only known the single-parent status in life, but some are in it for the first time — suddenly, like Samantha. Entering the single-parent world will require routine, organization, rules and discipline unlike any other lifestyle. Many readers may know of other instances of SIPS that have occurred for various reasons. The acronym was adopted as Samantha complained to her mother of the many challenges confronting her. "Sounds like SIPS to me," the grandmother quipped. The girls' grandmother lived close by and was able to help on occasion and offered valuable suggestions. Many a grandparent has taken children to raise after their own children have been out of the home for several years. The many changes since their children grew up may present the need for different rules and guidelines than the grandparents were accustomed to.

All single parents and single grandparents need to remember that a lot of help is available though a little research may be necessary to locate the help needed. Single parents are to be commended rather than put down. They are the primary influence of many children in America today. They need all the support we can give them.

Single Parents and Empty Nests

When a single parent's nest is empty it is really so, and may cause more of an adjustment than the single parent anticipates. Chances are the single parent already has a job so acquiring a job is not a cure. Several survey respondents revealed that they would refuse to date or to consider marriage until the children are out of the home. It appears to me that attitude is rarely going to help the children or the single parent. The "I live only for my children" attitude is going to be like a boomerang at some point. Single parents need to understand that they should continue to be the parent and never try to adapt the "brother or sister" relationship with children for several reasons. When the children are grown and leave home, the very empty nest causes the parent to suffer. Also if the parent's re-marriage has never been openly discussed as a possibility, jealously problems are a probability. This is a warning about being too close, too possessive, too involved with the children. If children are to reach adulthood with a healthy state of independence, parents must not smother them or be over-protective.

If a single parent is not considering remarriage, then certainly other ideas which have been considered in the past can now be pursued. The time of 'empty nest' is a good time to reevaluate life goals and ambitions. Most parents are still young enough when the last child leaves home to pursue a new career if that is their choice.

When the children are gone and if depression creeps in, the single parent can turn to other friends and relatives who have had a similar experience. The empty nest occurrence happens to all but may not be as frequently discussed as some other life events. Do not ruminate but act appropriately.

It is true that single parents have a big job, extra problems and a lot of challenges. Single parents can begin early in their career as single parents to take charge of their situation or they can waste precious years looking for someone to save them from their dilemma. I challenge all single parents to greet each day with a smile and a determination to better their lives with the best methods they can find and through it all, remember those occurrences they can put in their memory books. Life with teenagers will present special problems to the single parent family. Read about them in the next chapter, but first here is a poem about memories of a perfect day.

MEMORIES OF A PERFECT DAY

Children wrote their names in sand;
Driftwood stacked to make a fort;
Seaweed snarled around a log;
Every hole let sea come up;
Dreams were castles for that day;
Sea gulls swooped to catch their prey;
Grown-ups tried to stretch the time;
Dark clouds tried to hide the sun.

Names in sand will wash away;
Driftwood forts will disappear;
Seaweed snarled will come undone;
Holes will fill with sand again.
Dreams will change as time goes on.
Sea gulls always find their prey.
Grown-ups never stretch the time;
Dark clouds soon will float away.

Memories stand the test of time
Of perfect days and childish play.
I know now about life, tides, dreams,
Dark clouds, time and holes that fill up.

Marjorie Barton

TWELVE
LIFE WITH TEENAGERS

With the Hard-to-Find Teenager

When I voiced to a male business friend in Washington state that I didn't mind living alone he said I didn't have any right to say I lived alone because I had a teenage daughter still living at home. The man was single but had never lived with his teenage children and obviously was not aware of real life with a teenager.

I said that usually the only evidence that a teenager lived there was empty Coke cans and dirty clothes. The body was rarely present. As I said, "Alone with teenagers does not mean you are WITH anyone. It means you are alone most of the time without the presence of the beings whom you house, clothe and feed."

A teenager can pull a vanishing act faster than a professional magician. No sooner is a nice dinner at home planned and prepared than the teenager is no where to be found to enjoy it. In my case I knew that the daughter couldn't be too far away as she did not drive and the town was only two miles across at the widest point.

My daughter's excuses for sudden disappearances were many but easy to prove. She went for a walk after church with her friends. Or...she had to go clean Dale's apartment (her little paying job), or she got up while I went to church, ate a snack and went to practice volleyball.

The obvious problem was inconsideration or was it? If rules have not been made, they cannot be enforced. I knew that my casual, trusting attitude with Krystal was not for our best interests. I also knew that my single parenting skills were not as good as they should be, and my eratic hours as a newspaper publisher-editor did not help matters.

My problem was a simple problem compared to the problems of single parents' whose teenagers are roaming the streets in gangs or committing petty crimes at early ages. We had to work on better communication. I explained to Krystal a myriad of reasons why we should know each other's whereabouts. We agreed to leave a note in an appointed place as to our destinations when we could not give the message in person.

There must be rules. The right kind of rules help parents keep up with the teens so they know their whereabouts. The family meeting described in Chapter Eleven can be a big help in dealing with teenagers. Rules made in family meetings are easier to enforce than rules made by parents. The dictator attitude does not work well with teenagers of today. As is suggested by writer Joan Anderson, the family meeting should be regular, deal with new and old business, good news/bad news, weekend plans, and be followed by refreshments and family activity (89).

As friends are of utmost importance in the lives of teenagers, it is important that the friends feel welcome in the home. Teenagers need to understand that friends are welcome and at what time of day and for how long. If teenagers start out by introducing their friends to the parent, it will become a habit. Parents have a right to know parents of their children's friends and should not be reluctant to get that information. It is appropriate to use a phone call as a means of introduction. Parents of teenagers can help each other better when they have at least met on the phone. When the rules are clear, all parents know where their children are.

When driving becomes an issue, teenagers need to understand the limits and know what is expected of them. Involvement in SADD (Students Against Drunk Driving) may help the teenager deal with the temptations involved in driving and drinking. Curfews can be agreed upon during weekly meetings, but parents need to know the ordinances of their own community as well as their own personal preference.

According to Anderson, Alexander, and others, new single parents must be careful to be the parent, not just a friend (104,211-244). As was mentioned in the last chapter being "too close" or "too friendly" has its drawbacks. It can create a dangerous situation, because when the parent has to assert the parental role of correction or authority, the child often is rightfully confused. He thinks, "What happened to this Mom or Dad who was my best friend? Now she (or he) wants me to 'mind'. She acts like a dictator." It is nearly impossible to go from being a buddy to being the authority figure when the authority figure is needed.

Some who suddenly become single parents are confused about the new role they have acquired. Perhaps an effort to apologize for an unhappy situation that existed before becoming a single parent cause some to adopt the "pal" role. Parents have to be parents from the day one, if they expect to exert authority when it is seriously needed.

Keeping the Lines Open

The best way to encourage any child to be open with a parent is to take what the child says seriously and respond with respect. By the time teenagers are 14, they are making up their own minds about things, and all you can do is continue to present your values, your reasons, your life view in a calm and consistent manner and hope that you and your child can maintain an open line of communication.

As teenagers experiment to be one of the group, you can allow them to express their individuality through dress, hair, music ...and save your energy to fight larger battles, such as grades, drugs, and sex. Ms. Anderson said to go by the rule that as long as it doesn't hurt them or someone else, or violate your moral standards, they are free to experiment. She said to count yourself lucky, if experimentation is limited to hair, dress and dance or music (105). Do not feel threatened by the styles of the day, which should have nothing to do with your own standard house rules.

A teenager who is excessively quiet, withdrawn, doesn't say much, doesn't bring any friends home, and retreats to his room with loud music, may in trouble. If that teen goes out with friends but the parents do NOT know where he goes or what he does, he probably is or will be in trouble. A sure sign, according to all involved in drug use prevention, is when grades drop and school attendance is not satisfactory. If the quiet teen only stays at home and does not seem to be in trouble, he may be having a hard time adjusting to the demands of teen years.

All teens need to understand what parents' values are and that if they disagree, they will be able to establish their own set of values when they are independent and on their own. They need to understand that the parent still has love for them and that the parent is available.

If the teen actually seems depressed, help may be needed. In a world with ten or twelve million single parents with millions of teens, the number of possible situations runs into thousands. A single parent who is having a difficult time adjusting to the changes teenagers experience has help available in school counselors, physicians, police departments, drug testing centers, and books such as these mentioned. For parents who are having trouble controlling their children, ToughLove is an organization available. There is a book by the same name. Of course, parents find support from other parents in a similar situation and helpful options which have worked for other parents.

Single parents must remember that they do not have a monopoly on problems with teenagers. If teenagers are crying for attention, some acts of rebelliousness are their only means of gaining attention. If a teenager verbalizes his need for attention by complaining, the parent should certainly take a close look at his or her schedule and suggest a discussion or family meeting on the matter.

Those just embarking into the world of single parenting can be aware of the possibilities of the future and make efforts to avoid some calamities. If the new single parents have young children, planning ahead for the teen years may be helpful. In spite of the best efforts, open communication lines, religious background, and loving parents, some teens seem to make so many wrong choices they never recover. Others go through a stage of wrong choices and by the time they become parents have turned their lives around and become useful and caring parents.

Single parents reading this might profit from remembering their own teen years. Were parents too strict, too lenient, too absent, too indulgent, too wrapped up in their own affairs, or too busy? If today's single parents can remember the good and bad, right and wrong of their parents, perhaps they can build a better family framework that will follow the good or avoid the pitfalls of their own parents' mistakes.

Money and Teens

Parents have inadvertently been teaching their children about money all their lives, as Godfrey and Edwards explain, in two ways. One is unconsciously by example, and the other is consciously when an incident prompts an explanation. The young child usually at some point asks why can't something desired be purchased with a check or a credit card. While it is not necessary or proper to burden children with a parent's financial problems, they need not be kept totally in the dark. Children need to learn early that every desire of life will not be possible (13-15).

Children who are entering teenage earning years without established habits of money management will need training immediately. When a child starts earning money, he has an immediate assumption that he can control the spending. It makes sense, therefore, when a child says, "May I babysit (or mow the yard) for Mrs. X this afternoon, Mom?" that before Mom says yes, she needs to clarify the whole situation. Mom can say, "All right, but only if you agree for us to discuss your finances, because now you are probably going to earn money often." This leaves the situation open to discussion and is not a command from the parent. In many homes the earning of money by a teenager will force the teenager to consider how to spend, what to save, and in some cases, what to share or give to church or charities. It is never too early to have the teenager start saving for specialized training or education after high school.

Although teenagers don't have to know all the parent's finances, this would be a good time to explain "Mom's (or Dad's) budget." After a teen understands the parent's budget he will have a better concept and understanding of making one for himself, especially if he has a regular part time job. It would be an excellent time to show the teenager how a savings account earns money (by example, hopefully.) If a teen can see that Mom's 401K Savings Plan grew from $4,632.68 to $5,076.81 in one three-month quarter, the teen might be more interested in opening a savings account and watching his money grow.

As with all aspects of teenage years, money and the spending of it needs to be monitored. A parent, who thinks he or she is too busy to explain money matters to the teenager, will have no just reason to complain if the teen spends all his money on junk food and video tapes. The teen who thinks money doesn't matter is in for a rude awakening when he has to provide all his own needs if all the money blows off his money tree.

When Nancy* was a teenager, her parents were so busy running the family business it was easier to give her spending money every day as she asked for it, than to teach her any principles of how to use it. "I never had to ask for anything but one time," she explained, "and I know that wasn't right." It was very difficult for Nancy to be happy in a marriage that had much less materially than she was used to.

Teenagers can learn to use their money wisely, just as adults can. Guidance by example is good, but lessons in money management are as essential as lessons in the school building.

The Nightmare of Drugs and Alcohol

It has become obvious in recent years that the attempt to curb the drug and alcohol problems among teenagers has not been too successful. SAY NO TO DRUGS, SADD, MADD, D.A.R.E., may have lessened the impact in some towns, but the overall statistics have not improved. In recent years, one out of three 16 to 20 year old drivers who die in auto crashes had been drinking (Jones 118).

A survey by University of Michigan scientists, reported in a 1997 *Reader's Digest*, found that the proportion of eighth graders using illicit drugs had doubled since 1991. The reason, the scientists believed, is because schools, the media, and parents let their guard down (D'Aulaire 150).

The single parent who wants to defy statistics and raise children who are not on drugs or alcohol and are productive, reasonably well-adjusted adults must begin the effort early in the lives of the children. The parents must establish basic guidelines through education about all drugs, including nicotine, inhalants, and alcohol. Children cannot comprehend messages about what may be possible in the distant future. They are in life today and have a difficult time planning next year's school life, much less their health at age 40 or 50. If children could understand what happens to their brains and reflexes while they are using drugs they might be more concerned and more interested in refusing them.

Single parents not already in an drug educational effort pertaining to their children can begin as soon as they talk to the children on any subject. Many parents are unaware that even very young children might experiment with inhalants (Bartholomew 131-135).

A sad story can be told about Boyd*, whose father took him after a custody battle. Ironically, the father was able to win the court case because Boyd's mother's current husband drank too heavily. Boyd's father had all the right credentials and was as attentive as most busy fathers are. It could not be called neglect that Boyd sniffed gasoline with some of his junior high friends as an experiment. After some time Boyd became very depressed, suicidal, and required much psychiatric care. Boyd is now committed to an institution and will probably never be able to live on his own. This true story is only one of many similar ones.

When a parent explains to a child the dangers of poisons and household cleaners, he needs to carefully explain the dangers of sniffing any of several inhalants. The most often abused products include permanent-ink felt-tip markers, lighter fluid, adhesives, typewriter correction fluid, spray paint, paint thinners, gasoline and a wide range of aerosol products. According to a University of Michigan study, nearly 22 percent of the 18,000 eighth graders studied, admitted to trying inhalants at least once. Dying from use is far from the only danger. Vital organs, including the brain, are at risk. Unfortunately, there is a home page for teens on the Internet that provides instruction on where to get inhalants, how to use them, what to expect, but not how risky "huffing" is (Bartholomew 131-135).

The rules and results concerning drug use are the same for a single parent family as for a two parent family. A parent who smokes and drinks regularly in front of the children is sending a message of approval or at least a message of "there is no hurry, I'll stop some day." Experts seem to agree that it is acceptable for a child to see a parent drink alcohol, if it is only occasionally. If it is daily and the parent says he needs it "to relax" or "to cope with something," it is *NOT OK* (Hostettler 23-24).

Information about second-hand smoke and how parents who smoke influence their children to smoke is plentiful. Perhaps the greatest danger to children regarding the use of inhalants is adult denial, the insistence "my kid would never do that." Experts agree again that education is the key because no one would be able to bar a child's access to the hundreds of products that can be huffed to get high. A discussion on the issues of smoking, drinking, or using drugs must be on-going, but appropriate and not preachy. A follow-up discussion of an anti-drug commercial on TV is a good way to solicit opinions and feelings from children. If anti-drug education is not carried on in the local school district, the job is left entirely to family. A family must reinforce any anti-drug education the child learns from any outside source. Anti-drug education cannot be put off until it is convenient.

A specific family cited in the *Reader's Digest* article committed themselves to raising drug-free children. When the children were old enough to drive, the father made the promise that if either of his children did drink and drive, it would be the last time they would use the cars and that there would be no second chance (D'Aulaire 150-160).

Countries in the world with extremely low drunk driving rates use the same philosophy for all their drivers. There is no second chance. If a person is caught driving drunk, he will never have a license again. No one has explained why Americans are so indulgent of drunk driving.

Certainly a discussion of peer pressure and what it means to each child goes along with discussion about drugs and alcohol. A long-standing argument in the United States concerning the rampant use of drugs and alcohol is that the peer pressure is greater now than ever in history. The argument does not make an impression on those who believe that the stories of the Bible are true. According to the stories in the first five books of the Bible, peer pressure then was so great that God felt obligated to destroy the cities of Sodom and Gomorrah and earlier, someone led all the people to be so wicked that God caused the earth to be covered by flood. Another time a man named Moses went up a mountain to receive the Ten Commandments. When he returned, the people had stopped worshipping God and had melted all their gold, made a golden calf, and were having a great party (Genesis 7,19; Exodus 32). Peer pressure is no worse in today's world!

Peer pressure may be only one problem because the messages teens receive about drugs and alcohol may be confusing when they see something different in real life. When parents say that drinking will cause alcoholism but a sports figure who drinks still does well, that is confusing. When they have a friend who smokes pot but still makes straight A's, the contradiction makes the message unbelievable. Obviously the parent's knowledge and understanding about the drugs has to be clear.

In *10 Things Parents Should Know About Drugs and Alcohol Abuse*, the author Jep Hostetler explains ten things parents can do in the home. First, teach values, which he says parents must do before it becomes an issue. When prime-time TV shows people drinking alcohol, even though as hospitality, parents can discuss their values. As parents constantly teach values by what they do and say, they can actively talk about why they do what they do (60-61). Hostetler explains that self-centeredness is one cause of self-abuse, whether a person uses drugs, alcohol or food. Children can learn consideration and respect for others and usually do so by the example of their parents. He reminds that a sharing and caring attitude is a strong antidote to selfishness. As self-centeredness is one of the risk factors leading to self abuse, an opposite attitude may help lower the risk (99-122).

Others of the ten points include: doing things together, developing a sense of humor, giving responsibility, being good role models, agreeing on rules, learning to listen, maintaining fairness in conflicts, and learning all you can about alcohol and other drugs. Hostetler also gives ten specific suggestions for drug prevention on the community level (99-122). This book is a good one for in-depth ideas.

Teenage Pregnancy

The fact that the number of older women giving birth out of wedlock has increased, does not mean that the number of teens giving birth has decreased. In thirty years, the number of unmarried teens giving birth had increased from 17 per thousand to 46 per thousand (Chazin 49-52).

What is the role of the single parent preventing further increase in teen pregnancy? The trend of teen mothers has to stop or else the need for welfare assistance will continue to increase. Federal government efforts to cut back on welfare spending seem unlikely to succeed if teen pregnancies and drug and alcohol abuse continue to rise. All of those problem areas create extra spending by welfare agencies. Drug and alcohol treatment, as well as money for foster care of children in need, comes from government agencies. Dedicated single parents can make a difference.

Shoshana Alexander's book contains countless examples of single mothers and fathers who are accepting a challenge to raise children unencumbered by the memories of teen pregnancies and drug and alcohol problems. Communication on sex education has to begin at an earlier age than it did 50 years ago or perhaps, even 20 years ago. The need to establish communication lines with children begins at infancy and never ends until the parent or the child dies. Love and acceptance, not total approval, are the keys to communication.

Perhaps, but certainly not a sure thing, telling young teenage girls about the myths and realities of teen pregnancy might help. So many young girls think "we'll get married," but do not realize the changes and different stages of development all boys and girls go through before they reach adulthood. "We'll get married" is not a reality in at least 50 percent of the cases studied (Chazin 51).

The second myth, described in the same report, is "My baby and I don't need a man." As fewer than half the teens who gave birth out of wedlock marry within five years, obviously many children have no identifiable father. The children then are cheated out of having a dad as many teenage mothers realize too late (52). The third myth involves "I can still get an education and a good job." The reality is, according to the The Alan Guttmacher Institute, only 70 percent of the teens who had babies finish high school as compared to

90 percent of those who postponed childbearing. The institute also claims that the chance of attaining higher education is very slim (52).

The parents of teenage boys desperately need to educate their sons about teenage pregnancy and their roles as fathers. Relatively few marry the girl they made pregnant. Promiscuous boys need to stop and think what they are going to tell their son or daughter when he or she finds him and asks questions 20 or 30 years later. Boys should also be informed that the mother has a right to demand child support for the first 18 years and the money can be withheld automatically from the father's pay check if it is not given willingly.

Unfortunately the girl who bears the child still shoulders the major responsibility and that fact has not changed in 50 years. The rate of children born out of wedlock has steadily increased even with the advent of sexual knowledge and awareness programs. The problems will not go away easily.

Single Parents and the Future

Because divorce and death have touched such a larger percentage of families than in the far past and because most churches are playing a more active role in supporting singles, the future looks brighter. Approval may never occur but acceptance may become the norm. The arrival of the 21st century brings about more changes than any fiction writer could ever have imagined. Perhaps schools and families will see the need to teach about change and death and all the other areas in which significant problems have been noted.

Single parents for the most part, expect to find that reasonably compatible life mate at some point in the future. Preparing children for such a possibility is another responsibility. Single parents should socialize, both within the family group and on their own. Socializing in itself offers many teaching opportunities. Children as well as the single parent, have need of happy times which create happy memories.

Most important of all is that single parents help their children realize that they are significant and important in the world and that a single parent family is not necessarily a second-rate family, but a good and useful family. The role of various central and extended family members will be discussed in the next chapter.

THIRTEEN
LIFE'S NEW FAMILIES

Who Defined Family?

The marriage of one man and one woman who promise to remain faithful for life as husband and wife has been considered the basis for a family the past few centuries. The husband and wife were committed to one another for the purposes of mutual love and the raising of their children. A recent description of a traditional family has included the word "nuclear," meaning that which is the immediate family. When grandparents and other relatives are added the term becomes "extended" family. Today many families do not fit the original definition of "traditional" family.

A body of persons who live in one house and under one head has been considered a family. Any group with a tie of being related is a family. Two people living together and not tied by an official marriage may be considered a family by some. Often adopted or foster children are in a household and become part of a family, regardless of who is the head of the household. Probably more than 40 percent of the nation's households are non-traditional in the early connotation of the word.

Although no one argues the value of a stable, traditional family, the reality of the times is that it is best to prepare for alternative family life-styles. In addition to single parent problems already discussed, it must be noted that single parents frequently add sisters, brothers, nieces, nephews or grandparents to the household to form a "family."

Utilize Everyone

Preacher/writer Jerry Falwell listed socialization, security, support, encouragement, economics, and giving a sense of identity and belonging, as the reasons for families (47). Utilizing an extended family member can bring one or all of these characteristics into the structure of the family.

A widowed grandfather in the home might be the opportunity to provide a male figure for a fatherless home. A grandmother as well as a grandfather can help teach values and give care. Although grandparents may be independent longer than in years past, many still welcome the opportunity to share a home with children for economic reasons or for socialization. As children first learn many of life's lessons in the home during early years, stable, loving grandparents can enhance the learning. The more rapid changes of life-styles, values, and morals has made it very difficult for many grandparents to consider living with children. If three generations decide to or must live together, all generations need a clear understanding of rules and guidelines. Some compromising may be necessary by all but the older generation needs to be realistic about the differences of now and forty years ago. The younger generation also needs to be considerate of the elders as in playing loud music during late hours. A healthy grandparent likely will do nice things for the younger generation but should not be thought of as a free maid service.

With the career-oriented, never-married adults, whose numbers are growing, comes the opportunity for home-sharing. Two sisters, one a single parent and one not, are a possible combination for house mates. As family members experience divorce they often seek other family members for support and housing. The economics factor plays an important role in single guys "sharing expenses" with a married or single parent family member. An uncle in the home can allow a male role model for the children. As writer Ron Beathard said, "We make good uncles" (Referring to his never-married status 12).

Sharing homes is an economic advantage in most cases, but more frequently it is a means of building family relationships and providing stability when children are involved. Dr. Kevin Leman feels that the epidemic of dysfunctional families can be halted when families learn to put families first and return to establishing family values, in spite of the problems encountered in an age of rapid technological change. Putting job, church, a hobby, or a social life before family can and usually does undermine the strength of the family. Dr. Leman insists that family roots are important and explains that they provide stability, integrity, balance, and spiritual values. Dr. Leman emphasizes that children will only know about their roots if their parents tell them or show them pictures and records (12-14).

Grandparents Re-Emphasized

Don't forget the grandparents. Grandparents should not be expected to take over child-rearing because of failed marriages, but grandparents on both sides of the family can be especially stabilizing to children in a single parent family. The relationship between parents and children is naturally unstable as the child grows into adulthood. A caring grandparent can be a Great Parent forever — so long as a vital connection is established early in a child's life. The vital connection is developed by shared time and intimate contact, that which comes naturally for most grandparents.

Authors Arthur Kornhaber and Kenneth L. Woodward explain that the connection between grandparents and grandchild is second in emotional power only to the bond between parent and child. Grandparents who deny themselves the pleasure of grandparenting are also weakening the foundation blocks of their families (Chapter 2).

The new families of today need grandparents reinstated, as sorely as the grandchildren need them. Many grandparents are self-sufficient yet are saddened by the distance to which the family circle has grown. Most of them manage visits although perhaps not as often as they would like. Most grandparents enjoy visits but not too many want their freedom spoiled by taking on grandchildren to parent. As the telephone is so widely used today, financially secure and concerned grandparents can at least establish telephone connections with grandchildren who live far away.

Concerning the importance of roots, Dr. Kevin Leman said that too many families have sacrificed something very valuable in the name of chasing the great American dream. Leman said when he was interviewed about the desirability of living in Sunbelt country (Arizona) he said he thinks that young couples today should live as close to one set of grandparents as possible. He said that was his only comment about living in the Sunbelt. In other words, in moving across the country for a "better job" a lot of intangibles can be lost (14).

Families of all combinations need a grandparent. When marriages break up or a long distance move takes place, these things need to be explained to children (Ch 2). It is well documented in *Grandparents, Grandchildren* that children feel wounded if the bond is broken and never acknowledged. It is as if some vital part of themselves was missing. Another aspect of grandparenting is the "Sunday dinner at grandmother's house. When the grandparents are available the dinner table remains important in family life. The roles of the grandparents vary but usually include the grandparent as a teacher, a caretaker, a negotiator between child and parent, as a same-sex role model, and as a connection between the past and the future (143).

Grandparents and their behavior often determine how young people feel about the old people in society. An active grandparent can cause a grandchild to picture old age as nothing to be feared, and the grandparent is not thought of as "old." On the other hand some children expressed their feelings that a grandparent who does nothing, only moving around very little, would have been able to do more except that he or she just stopped being active.

The mobility of both adult children and their parents may have created an impact on the third generation not yet fully realized. To counteract the absence of grandparents, some families "adopt" an older neighbor or a friend to play the grandparent role. They realize their children as well as the older person have much to offer each other. This is a strongly recommended solution in the "scattered family society" in which people live today.

Long Distance Parents

Another aspect of unique families concerns a parent who does not live nearby and any parenting done is by long distance. Children whose mother or father lives far away should understand that even two-parent families can have a parent who is away part time and that it is important and all right to like the non-custodial parent.

As Miriam Galper Cohen explained in *Long Distance Parenting*, children learn about themselves based on their relationships with their parents. A child's relationship with a parent is a living, breathing thing. She reminds that the parent-child bond is deep and as observed in the re-uniting of adopted children and parents, years of absence erase quickly (176-178).

Achieving a successful relationship from a long distance takes commitment and cooperation from both parents. Ms. Cohen says the single main ingredient of the successful relationship is continuity. The child needs to know when he will hear from the parent again. Both parents need to understand that the long-distance relationship will not develop overnight, but that it will take time. Children and parents have to learn to talk about little details of life, including feelings. The discussion of feelings may not be easy but the parent needs to be open while allowing the child to do so, also. Time invested in establishing confidence, trust, and dependability will reap rewards (20-39).

Although there may be as many non-traditional families as traditional families, the various members of the non-traditional families, whether living under the same roof or not, can each play important roles in the development of the children in their care. Each person in the family can teach and give, according to his or her ability.

Gifts to Give and Lessons to Teach

Certain gifts can be bestowed on children, regardless of how many parents they have, whether they have one single, one step, one adopted, one remarried, or one never married parent. The opportunity to develop a vital connection to one or more grandparents can be counted a gift. The willingness of a single mother to develop a friendship with a child's father so the father can give the child a relationship only he can provide, is a gift. The same is true of the mother-child relationship. Everyone in the family must cooperate to make these gifts possible.

Creating situations that make good indelible memories may be a gift less labeled than many but essential to happy adult lives. Happy children are usually happy adults. Happiness is the stuff of which memories are made. Happiness usually occurs within incidents that have no material or monetary value such as an annual trek to a grandparents' home in the country with unlimited play time in woods and hills nearby. Camping trips to nearby parks, rivers, lakes, and woods or just a day trip to a nearby creek or river to play along the edge can produce those happy memories. Gifts such as these usually require time and little else. Single parents must ask themselves which is more important: cleaning house and doing laundry or taking time with children outdoors? A promised short trip may produce more cooperation for completion of household tasks.

As if single parents don't have enough to do, the reminder of all the intangible lessons they need to teach their children is overwhelming. It does not take a long time to make a list of lessons to be taught.

Children may be born optimistic, believing they can do anything but parents may inadvertently teach them they cannot. Negative vibes start in the cradle, when a mother says, "Stop wiggling, I can't change your diaper." For some mothers and fathers the vibes never stop. The message, "You can't go to college because we don't have the money," may be the final message Susie and Johnny need to set off into a world of non-achievement.

Single parents probably know without being reminded that they are the most effective role models for their children in all things, including moral and spiritual values. Parents can help build self-esteem in not so thin children and self-reliance and independence in all. Parents must guide children in how to act properly to dispel depressive thoughts. Sadly, girls have been brainwashed that thin is best and boys tend to use alcohol and drugs as a coping outlet for any of their short-comings (of course some girls do too). Parents CAN help their children in this matter.

Children can be taught a healthy balance of positive thinking just the same as adults. Most children can be helped to grow into resilient, useful, optimistic adults. It usually does take some help from an adult; few come out of bad beginnings without an adult role model somewhere in life. Rather than spend time being overly concerned with your non-traditional family, be concerned with loving every minute of life.

Preparing for Another Family

Famous last words of divorced or widowed people are "I'll never marry again." Of the divorced population, most remarry at least once (Census). Regardless of the family arrangement today, every family should prepare its members for possible change of marital status in the future.

Henrietta* was an active participant of a singles group in her west Texas community. She said, "I hate to date someone who says 'I'll never marry again'. I have dated three men who proclaimed that so emphatically and within six months, they were married. I take it as a reverse statement now. They should say, 'I'm going to marry the one who catches me!"

Singles of all ages sometimes opt for living together without marriage because they have misconceptions about marriage changing attitudes. The "everything was all right until we married" statement doesn't say much for basic attitudes and/or compatibility and says very little about communication.

Single parents concerned about the effect of "live-in" relationships on the children should consider a study conducted by the Philadelphia Child Guidance Clinic. With 87 mothers who had custody of their children, the children fared best when the mother was not seriously romantically involved, and worst of all when the mother was living with a man but unmarried (Anderson 284).

The researchers did not recommend sudden change in single parent families but careful consideration before remarrying. It is a mistake to marry for social, legal or financial reasons, or to recruit a father for the children. The quality of the relationship has to come first. Ms. Anderson says that there must be realistic expectations about a newly, blended family to dispel the myths. Instant family love or a similarity to the first biological family or that a new parent can make up for the defects of the missing parent are facts not likely to occur (285-289).

Single parents with young children need to remind themselves that there are no perfect princes or princesses. Any new family arrangement will take time and effort to make it work, make it peaceful, and make it happy. It will not happen overnight. Jealousy among all members of a newly blended family is common and the basis for the jealousy needs to be faced head on and dispelled. Dislikes among the new family unit can be softened and/or accepted. A new stepmother can take the advice of the experienced by looking hard for something to like, then praising the person for the attribute, then looking for something else and add to the list of likes until the unlikable can be accepted. The probability of a single parent family becoming a two-parent family again is in the statistical truth that the majority of divorced people remarry and never-married single parents usually marry. The divorce rate peaked in 1978, then dropped and has been level for more than a decade (Census). The singles living in the double world need to make positive plans for living single, yet be aware that they might return to the double world.

Avoiding Media Scare Tactics

When a single parent reads that children in families such as theirs have higher crime rates, receive less educational opportunities, have more children out of wedlock or any such negative information, it is time to reverse the trend by doing something counteractive in their own home. Singles, one by one with planning and determination can help change the statistics.

Sara McLanahan of Princeton University reported in Parents magazine that she hoped to prove that single mothers can do as good a job of raising children as two-parent families because she had been a single mother for ten years. She was disappointed in her findings. Children of single parent families have a higher school dropout rate. The children have lower grade point averages and poorer school attendance records. As a adults they are less likely to graduate from college and more likely to become single parents themselves. These are averages but the warnings are clear(18). Each single parent family has its own particular problems. The parent should seek advice and help if he or she wants to improve the lives and futures of the children in the home. Single parents should become part of the effort to improve the sad statistics.

Families can be found with many combinations of men, women and children and another growing segment of population in the U. S. are single seniors. As life-expectancy continues to increase, the number of single seniors will likewise. A look at their new attitudes and life-styles is next.

FOURTEEN
LIFE WITH SINGLE SENIORS

It would be unfair to write about living single in a double world and never make mention of those who have reached official senior status of 65 years. This is in praise and concern for the eleven million who have never-married and another fourteen million are left alone after death or divorce. Forecasts of longevity tell us that number will increase dramatically over the next thirty years.

Although life for single seniors may be tough at times, it is nonetheless quite improved from a century ago. Middle to lower socio-economic senior singles of a century ago could expect little except to go to the "poor farm" or live with children. Many counties actually operated a "farm" which was a home, usually in a rural setting where people could go who had no other home or financial aid. I remember my mother's church missionary group taking food and clothes to the "poor farm."

Few single seniors of today have only the choices of living with someone or living on a poor farm. The availability of Social Security insurance, Medicare/Medicaid and other planned retirement programs has allowed a bigger percentage of seniors to be less dependent on others for living arrangements and medical help.

Because of the greater opportunities for independent living, most seniors who become single again are better able to cope. Those who have always been single also have much more to look forward to in later years than did those of a century ago. Most never-married seniors are happy people. Many own their own homes and pursue their interests and hobbies. Some who have been married a long time perceive these never-married people to be extremely different. As has been discussed in other chapters, they are not different except for being single. Therefore why have we created such a gap in our thinking?

It is true that many single seniors live on a very low fixed income with little chance to do much more than exist. I certainly do not claim to have any magic answers for those people. Certainly many have struggled their whole lives to make ends meet and come to the last part of life with little to look forward to. However, many who have had little have adjusted and are not unhappy. The main concern will be paying for needed medical care. If they can gain any insight from this book, I am glad.

Single seniors with less than adequate material possessions have free services such as those found in libraries which includes large print books and videos to borrow, if the senior has a VCR.. Most small towns have active senior centers but I cannot speak for the very big cities. Single seniors of means should try to help less fortunate single friends in every way possible.

One way to help those less fortunate is through volunteering. An awareness of the plight of older people living alone is often brought to the attention of service organizations and church groups. Single seniors often benefit from volunteer programs by getting their house painted or repaired. Volunteers often transport seniors to doctor's appointments. Perhaps caring groups everywhere will soon make sure that less people suffer unnecessarily from inadequate care or inadequate medicine supply.

The age of volunteerism seems to have enveloped the United States, indeed, perhaps the world. With a knowledge of any catastrophe in any location, rescue teams and Red Cross and other organizations are quick to help. An effort to teach the act of volunteering is evident in many schools of today, even required in some college classes. Perhaps the efforts to teach volunteering and community service will eventually be of great help to the growing senior population.

A challenge for those who promote volunteering would be to make and maintain a list of everyone who lives alone in every community, at least those categorized as seniors. Apparently the percentage of the population living alone has increased without recognition. I live on a block with seven houses, two of which are occupied by only one person.

New Choices for Single Seniors

There are many new choices for single seniors concerning housing, medical needs and activities. A new magazine by that name New Choices caters to people over 50. Let's take a look at new options.

Housing complexes exist with several options in housing. Those who have lived in a large house can opt for a condo or an apartment where they may have secured admittance, no lawn care and no maintenance costs. Other senior housing often includes mobiles in a park which includes an activity center and other amenities. When a person needs assistance in living, other options which include meals and cleaning services in the same big complex are sometime available. The next and last step would be a nursing home in the event it is needed. I do know of planned complexes with all of the above.

If a person's health is deteriorating yet not to the stage of needing full time nursing care, some facilities offer various levels of "assisted living."This arrangement usually includes a nurse on staff but is not a nursing home, where the person requires continual medical services. There is a great deal of variation in services provided as some similar places expect residents to come and go, yet have a curfew. This type of living arrangement allows the single person to maintain some independence, while being assisted in housekeeping and/or nutritious meal provisions.

Single seniors whose fixed income is rather low and who may be having a hard time with finances should investigate low-cost housing. Even if the waiting list seems a long time, such as a year or more, single seniors should put their names on the waiting list. Low cost housing can certainly help ease the problems of paying for medicines and other medical needs not covered by Medicare.

All seniors now have the option to be on Medicare or in a Health Maintenance Organization (HMO) which utilizes Medicare in a different way and is less expensive than a Medicare Supplement. This requires careful consideration. A single senior who does not understand all the implications should call more than one insurance agent to have it explained. An HMO may fit your needs but you need to understand it well. A single senior on an exceptionally low fixed income should see if he or she qualifies for medical care in addition to Medicare (Medicaid). The rules vary from state to state and from year to year.

I used to jokingly say that I would go to a Senior Center when I get old and do not have activities to keep me busy. (You don't have to be 65 to attend). Actually I certainly commend senior centers and their role in the lives of seniors. A single senior can find companionship and often very helpful advice in the form of special speakers. Other special services are presented to senior centers that might be overlooked on a one to one basis. Most senior centers have regular dances, regular meals, activities such as quilting and ceramics, pool tables, designated table game hours (pinochle, bridge) and other special times.

To say that senior singles have no special needs is untrue and unfair. Of course they do. Just because a person is past 65 or 70 or even 75 does not mean that they have less need for conversation and activities than a younger single. The support groups often appear in a different format and have different activities than a younger group would have. For example line dancing is quite popular with senior singles. In some communities lessons are offered by various organizations as a service and charge no fee. It is certainly good aerobic exercise in a rather painless fashion.

Senior centers have been known to arrange for hearing tests, regular blood pressure tests and other minor medical preventive care services. Single seniors who do not use a senior center should be supportive of it because they may be very glad it exists, as they may want to use it some day.

Retire with a Purpose

Single seniors who have found no hobby or who are physically and emotionally spent from caring for an ill spouse need to regroup and add a new purpose to life. Although we may tend to think of hobbies as knitting or woodcraft or flower gardens or cooking, volunteering can be the hobby that fits the needs of many. Discovering that you are 65 or more and suddenly alone after a long life with a spouse is bound to require major adjustment. Relief that a long illness is over is not always as sustaining as some thought it would be. Retiring after a life of singlehood but without developing adequate substitutes for a career could be just as devastating. Any younger singles or even couples reading this book should take note and begin to plan life for the Golden Years as it has been dubbed, recognizing that it might be spent alone.

Those Glorious Years

Many people look forward to retirement in eager anticipation of travel, pursuing hobbies and just doing what they want to do when they want to do it. Others approach that time of life with little to look forward to except ominous medical bills and the possibility of ending life in a nursing home. The variation of the activities of retirement years is as many as there are people. It is sad that some have little choice, partly because of lack of pre-retirement preparation and partly because of life's earning abilities. How people face the last years of life varies tremendously.

Take for example Ruby Walker of Muskogee, OK. Ruby has been a widow for about 30 years and is an example that money doesn't buy happiness. At 77 Ruby was still cleaning houses, but relaxes in her garden. Her flower garden is 110 X 120 and full of many wildflowers as well as a 100 different colors of irises. As Ruby spends many hours tending her flowers she finally started charging a small amount for a start of a plant. She loves to share her flowers with her church, where she takes a bouquet every Wednesday and Sunday nearly all year around (Muskogee Daily Phoenix).

I have had a friend since childhood who is never-married. She is retired from a career in government service and lives in our home town of Muskogee. Betty is a very active single senior, who can't find time to do everything she wants to.

A widow in the same town is a life-long personal friend, who always seemed like an aunt to me. Euna Featherston said recently that she assumed when Charlie died that she wouldn't be here very long. That was nearly 20 years ago. She does not despair of her life but has enjoyed most of those years watching grandchildren and great-grandchildren grow and enjoying her church.

On a recent birthday Euna was presented with a quilt on which patches depicted activities or interests of various grandchildren and great-grandchildren. Until recently she attended church in person. Now she attends via television. Her sense of humor is outstanding and another book of mine is sprinkled with some of her stories. If only all single seniors could have such an attitude and such an interest in living. At 93 plus, she still lives alone (Euna died during the final edit of this book).

My next door neighbor Wanda Smart has been a widow only a short time. She does volunteer work at her church and takes part in many activities. She walks at least three miles most mornings and has adjusted well after a 50 year marriage. Wanda said that friends and her church have been important to her recovery. She also said that it helps to be unafraid. As mentioned elsewhere caution is important but no need to be overly afraid.

Another single friend of mine in Washington state had been a widow about a year when I first met her. Camille Neubert belonged to a Loners on Wheels group (RV travel), danced at senior centers at every opportunity, sang in her church choir, did a tremendous amount of outdoor work and kept an immaculate home. She did a lot of volunteer work at her local senior center in Twisp, WA. Busy, yes; and you would never guess her age (then 75) by her appearance or her activity.

Wood Whatley of Quanah, Texas, is one of my favorite single seniors. He has now outlived his wife by 14 years. He is mentioned several times in this book because he is so active he puts many younger seniors to shame. He has always said that if you quit being active you will die sooner (He is 98 at this writing).

Most active single seniors will tell you that to sit and wait is to die young. I recently read about a woman who has been blind most of her life. She taught in a school for the blind, but in her thirties she also began experiencing a loss of hearing. Persistence, a will to overcome, tenacity, can all be used to describe this woman who consults and solves problems on her computer that people with sight and hearing cannot. She is 65 but has no reason to stop doing what she loves to do and what a service she is to others. She lives with a sister.

A portrait artist in New York City named Gloria Schumann who painted President Richard Nixon's inaugural portrait was invited to come to Muskogee, Oklahoma, to do a portrait of a child of the Griffin family. The Griffin's owned a cannery and later a television station. The hospitality of Muskogee was so impressive that when Mrs. Schumann came to do another portrait the next year she decided to move to Muskogee.

Mrs. Schumann had been a widow since 1956, when at that time, she vowed if her husband did not recover from his lengthy illness she would never remarry. Her New York friends tried to convince her she would never find enough work in Muskogee, but she moved anyway. Her life reads like a story book. Indeed, she is a single senior who is still doing portraits and further proof of the value of purpose in life (Muskogee Daily Phoenix, Dub West Column). We do not have to be outstanding artists or craftsmen to have a rewarding life, but living life with a purpose will enhance the living.

SINGLE SENIORS TAKE CARE, BEWARE!

As many accidents can be avoided, so could many instances of crime. It is no longer true that strangers can be welcomed into homes. It behooves everyone to read all articles they notice pertinent to scams and how strangers often gain entrance to a home. Singles alone especially need to use special precautions in malls, parking lots, and general travel. Singles should always lock car doors, park in well-lighted areas and have the key in hand to unlock a car door. When reservations are made at motels, singles should request a lower floor, leaving less opportunity for problems getting to and from a room.

Some single seniors work well past the age of 65. Those who work night shifts or who leave work after dark can demand an escort to their car if they are afraid or if the parking lot is not very well lighted. It is not a good idea to walk to a car alone any place after dark. Do not be a martyr.

Single senior Betty Lou* had no laundry equipment at home but seldom locked her car when she took clothes in and out of the laundromat. After she read of an instance of murder when someone hid in the back seat while a person was in a laundromat, she always locked her car when she was doing her laundry. Simple acts of precaution can discourage possible crime.

Romance for Single Seniors

Many widows and widowers past 65 spent most of their adult life married. They may often say, "I'm not interested in a romantic relationship, but I would like a companion." They see a new companion as someone with whom to share time, retirement, projects and who would create a couple again. Unfortunately everyone does not reveal his or her honest feelings while dating. A woman who says she isn't interested in romance because she had a long, happy marriage doesn't always say, "I would marry for companionship," even if it is true.

That single seniors are incapable of or have no business being romantic is a thought that should have disintegrated about 50 years ago when life expectancy began to increase so dramatically. Ask any active senior how old they feel and the answer may surprise you unless you are already the same age and feel very young. When my mother was about 75 she remarked that she didn't feel old but her bones did not want to cooperate with her mind. She had arthritis in a bad way.

It does not matter how old I am chronologically, I think I am at least 20 years younger and expect to continue behaving that way for a long time. I have met many single seniors whose age you would never guess. Activity and attitude plus a healthy life style have usually been important factors in the lives of older people who do not "look their age."

Adult children often feel a widowed parent is being untrue to the deceased spouse when a mid-life mom or dad marries again. In cases of this type the adult children need to examine the situation carefully. If money and property are not an issue in the marriage, the adult children need to consider the happiness of the older adults and strive to be friends in the situation. No one replaces a deceased parent, but generally the new spouse just wants to be friends with the step-children, although they accept the parent role when invited. The increased life expectancy in the United States makes it probable that a healthy widow or widower might live many years alone if they do not remarry.

Planning for Senior Years Alone

If you are not a senior and reading this, take heart.

If you have a single senior parent, reconsider all your attitudes concerning the senior years. If you have a single senior parent, perhaps it is time to help them plan for a long life just as you need to plan for yours.

When a person of today reaches 65 and has no major

health problems the life expectancy increases dramatically. It is acceptable and in most cases the desire of the single senior to want to live alone as long as possible. Many would not even consider a marriage, while others hope for that very thing. Encouraging seniors to develop hobbies and interests not dependent on a couple life is certainly a wise undertaking for adult children or friends.

For seniors who haven't given a thought to living alone perhaps it is time to give that issue serious consideration. The most certain aspect of life is change. Those old jokes about the only certain thing being death and taxes are sadly true. Seniors should not have any guilty feelings about planning what they might do or have to do, when and if they find themselves alone with years of life left to live. Singles of all categories can plan and adapt and protest when appropriate, but there are a few promises they can hold on to. Tune in your mind scanner for a look at promises we can rely on in the next chapter.

FIFTEEN

LIFE'S PROMISES!

Promises of Laws

The laws of this land are full of promises. Consider the Bill of Rights. Singles should use their right to free speech, free press and the right to protest. It is time for singles to stand up and be counted.

Because singles and couples often change status more than once in life, it isn't feasible to join a single group assuming it will be for life. Membership in organizations such as DAR (Daughters of American Revolution), the American Legion or a lodge can be forever. However, singles could and should ban together to eliminate the many unfair practices cited earlier in this book and many that have not been mentioned. Power exists in numbers. Singles should let their numbers be known and help create a better acceptance of their status.

Americans have much freedom of choice and that includes the right to live alone, remain single and pursue any legal job or pastime without being questioned or criticized. The age of job stereotyping should have gone out with the horse and buggy. The stereotyping *IS* less than 50 years ago. A man can be a nurse and a woman can be a doctor. A man can be a secretary and a woman can be a mechanic. A man can be a single parent and do a good job. Those are a few examples.

More examples of progress in less stereotyping are seen when a woman is an executive of a company. A single person can be president, but do you realize how few have been? Singles of the United States could unite and easily elect a president. Single women could probably do it without the aid of single men if they all voted. (That is because our voting record as a nation isn't very admirable.) Times have changed but prejudices have not disappeared.

Freedoms have different meanings than they did 200 years ago. Some approve of the changes; some don't. The freedoms mentioned here have nothing to do with morals. They often have to do with survival in an age of rapidly advancing technology. Promises of protection in the freedoms in America is unlike any other country. Singles must latch on to the promises and create a better image of single life. Many discrimination laws on record are difficult to enforce. Do you ever see a credit application which does not ask for a spouse's name?

God's Promises

God did not promise that skies would always be blue or that it would never storm, nor did He promise that life would always be easy and that there would be no tears or hard times. He did promise to be present if we allow Him.

In the Bible there are many promises. Biblical promises are a little different from government promises in that they seem to be true if you the person choose to believe. Take for example Psalms 121:2, "My help comes from the Lord, which made heaven and earth." If you do not believe that God made heaven and earth you will not consider biblical promises to be of any help. If you believe, then finding such assurance in the Bible may indeed help in times of trouble. The God of the Bible does not promise that there will be no trouble in life, He merely promises to be there when it arrives.

"How can you bear up after such hardships in your life?" Many a single person has been asked that question after losing a spouse who experienced a devastating, painful illness before death and perhaps lost a parent during the same time frame. A person who relies on God's promises might say, "You know — I have a peace that passes understanding, it's one of God's promises." (Phillipians 4:7)

In a recent local news feature which spoke of dealing with suicide, one person had written about suicide because it had happened twice in her family. First her husband, then her son had committed suicide. She claimed that she and her son had not dealt with her husband's suicide. She said that it is not good to pretend something never happened. Her son's method of coping was to do the same thing her husband did — commit suicide. How could she live with such tragedy? Perhaps she said, "I have strength for all things in Christ who empowers me."(Phillipians 4:13) She was trying to make others aware that such a tragedy must be dealt with if it occurs.

Single parents can find promise in a well known proverb of the Bible which states, "Train up a child in the way he should go; and when he is old, he will not depart from it." (Proverbs 22:6) Singles looking for a spiritual type of leadership may want to heed another proverb which says, "Trust the Lord with all thine heart; and lean not unto thine own understanding. In all they ways acknowledge him, and he shall direct they paths. (Proverbs 3:5,6)

Stories abound of successful people who were raised by a single parent. As singles read such stories, they should let that knowledge help them to know that being married is not a necessary factor in raising fine children.

Singles who complain or who just openly say they have no one with whom to discuss their problems may find a lot of guidance in studying the Bible. A psychology professor once told a class I attended that the Bible was probably the best book on psychology available and not used as often as it should be. Here again is another point in favor of attending a group Bible study: for the guidance which might be obtained.

Hope for the 21st Century

Hope for the 21st century will come about if singles can make the world aware of the growing number of singles.

Married people may acquire different attitudes only when they become aware and learn about the idiosyncrasies of living single. More married people will become aware of the dilemmas which both the married and the singles face as personal involvement becomes more and more common. Soon nearly every family will have one or more single children or another close relative who is single. As this occurs and education takes place, all can react toward each other with more understanding.

Another form of hope for singles comes in the fact that issues of singledom are being faced head on rather than hid in some dark corner, never to be mentioned. The Singles Center on computer internet systems appears to be calling attention to unfair practices in every aspect of living. (Chapter Two) It always takes a lot of unrest and complaints before any wrongs are made right. Issues involving singles will be no different.

Problems are just challenges for the day and being single often adds to the problems. It is time for singles to take a firm stand with friends, relatives and even married friends who try to use pressure to get the single to change his or her lifestyle (as in, find someone to marry, because it is acceptable.)

In *The Road Less Traveled* the author, M. Scott Peck, said that we need to accept responsibility for a problem before we can solve it. Every individual must face his or her own problems; as everyone else is busy solving his own. Being left alone by death or divorce, and/or also being a single parent will present myriads of problems to all involved. This is all part of life and the inevitable changes that must come in it.

Solving the problems confronting singles is one more reason why singles *SHOULD* be involved with other singles. There are enough adult singles to sway almost any election in the United States. Some issues such as discrimination in housing, taxes, travel and the work place can be dealt with by legislation. Other issues concerning attitudes and misunderstandings must be dealt with through the education of the double world. If women could gain the right to vote and factories could be stopped from hiring children and women can be in the military then likewise, singles can have a voice in all that concerns them.

All who read this book should vow to apply what they have learned so that the gap between singles and doubles will be lessened. Those who are married should vow to not only be friendly but to try a little socializing with some of the singles they already know.

It is time to advance into the next century with attitudes that keep up with technology. If computers can be so amazing, why should we allow our brains to drift so far behind? It is time to unite rather than divide. Far too many single people live in our country for the happily married couples to pretend they do not exist. An attitude of "I guess they like being alone all the time" is not an appropriate or caring statement for anyone to make.

It is past time for singles to speak out, be heard, be noticed and be understood. Singles must do their part to clear up unnecessary mis-concepts of living single.

In the meantime those re-entering or already in the single world should realize they are far from alone. Those singles who have problems adjusting to single life have more sources of help than in the past. Singles have better probability of establishing good credit, saving for retirement, owning a home and other advantages nearly unheard of half a century ago.

Attitudes have changed slightly in the double world. Discrimination is slightly less; but the progress is slow. Progress is neither all encompassing nor universal. Progress in non-discrimination and better attitudes by the general public is spotty, but it is progress. Progress in solving problems of living single will take work. The problems of living single will not go away by ignoring them. If a single realizes he or she is the victim of any discrimination because of marital status, the single person must speak up. Hopefully a general change of attitude will come about in the 21st century.

Let us adapt, adjust, smile, plan and speak up when appropriate, but most of all let us live with pride and joy if we live single in this double world.

Appendix

Questionnaire for Living Single in a Double World

FOR NEVER MARRIED

1. Do you ever observe different treatment, because you are single? Give examples

   A: In the workplace:

   B: Socially

   C. At church or community organizations

2. Do you ever hear comments deriding, questioning, or sympathizing with your status as a single person? Give examples

3. Can you give any examples of discrimination that have occurred, because of your single status? (jobs, credit, on job positions)

4. Does the idea of "commitment" frighten you, or can you state clearly why , if you prefer to be "single"?

5. State advantages and disadvantages to being single, according to your own experiences.

IF YOU WISH TO MAKE OTHER COMMENTS, DO SO. FEEL FREE TO USE THE BACK OF THE QUESTIONNAIRE, AND RETURN IN ENCLOSED ENVELOPE. NO NAMES WILL BE USED IN BOOK, BUT FOR STATISTICAL PURPOSES, Check:
AGE GROUP: UNDER 30____ 30-50____ Over 50____
MALE____ FEMALE____
LIVE IN: Town under 10,000____
Town 10,000 - 100,000____ CITY OVER 100,000____

INCLUDE YOUR NAME AND ADDRESS, IF YOU WISH TO BE NOTIFIED OF PUBLICATION OF THIS BOOK QUESTIONNAIRE FOR LIVING SINGLE IN A DOUBLE WORLD

Additional Comments

FOR WIDOWS AND WIDOWERS

1. Can you describe some of your emotions/reactions, when you first knew you had lost your spouse?
2. Did you think you were prepared for events that took place soon after your spouse died?
3. Do you recall any inappropriate remarks or incidents which took place at that time?
4. Do you recall any very helpful remarks or incidents, which took place soon after your spouse's death?
5. Did you become involved with a "support group"?
6. Have you had any experiences, which clearly indicate that you would have been more comfortable...or accepted, if you were still part of a couple?
7. Can you give any examples of feeling ill at ease socially, or at work or church?
8. Did you have any financial or credit problems that seemed to surface because of your marital status?
9. Can you share anything, which might help others adjust to "single life"?
10. Have you read any books, which have been particularly helpful?
11. Make any comments you wish, in addition to answering the questions. Use the back of the questionnaire, if necessary.

No real names or places will be used in the book. Use the return envelope. And for statistical purposes, Please:

Male____ Female____

Age group - Under 30____ 30-50____ Over 50____

Town size: Under 10,000____ 10,000 to 100,000____ Over 100,000____

IF YOU WISH TO BE NOTIFIED OF THE PUBLICATION OF THIS BOOK, PLEASE ENCLOSE YOUR NAME AND ADDRESS.

SINGLE BY DIVORCE

1. When you first divorced, what was your emotionally reaction?
2. Can you recall reactions of friends and relatives?
3. Were you surprised at your own reactions, and/or the reactions of others? Comment:
4. Can you describe any financial or credit problems you experienced?
5. Can you recall your feelings about going places you formally went "as a couple"? (social, church, school events)
6. If you were also a single parent, can you relate problems special to being a "single parent"?
7. Did you seek a support group? If yes, describe and relate benefit or lack of benefit?
8. Did you have to, or did it seem necessary to find new friends? If so, how did you do this?
9. What have you done to help your children (single parents) overcome the problems you confronted?
10. Make any comments you wish about sex and commitments, and remarriage and/or relationships. Use the back of the questionnaire, if necessary, mail in the enclosed envelope.

No real names will be used in the book. FOR STATISTICAL PURPOSE ONLY:

Male____ Female____

Under 30____ 30-50____ Over 50

Town Size: Under 10,000____ 10,000-100,000____

Over 100,000____

IF YOU WISH TO BE NOTIFIED OF THE PUBLICATION OF THIS BOOK, PLEASE ENCLOSE YOUR NAME AND ADDRESS.

Epilogue

Yes, upon a glance, you will know that everyone, single or married, needs to abide by these ABCs. However, it has always seemed to me that we singles could adapt better to single life if we tried harder to use these guidelines.

A - **Articulate** (what you feel), **Avoid** (pessimists), **Acclimate** (to a new life), **Accentuate** (the positive)

B - **Bury** (the past), **Beautify** (your surroundings), **Balance** (your checkbook carefully), **Budget** (wisely)

C - **Communicate** (or learn to, if you don't), **Cry** (but not forever), **Circulate** (make new friends), **Change** (whatever makes you feel better)

D - **Discover** (what you've missed), **Dismiss** (bad thoughts), **Delight** (in all the goodness of life), **Dazzle** (your friends with a positive attitude)

E - **Evaluate** (yourself, your job, your lifestyle), **Enthusiam** (put it in your voice, walk, attitude)

F - **Friend** (be one, someone needs YOU), **Fumigate** (your mind, if it needs cleansing), **Fend** (off negatives, you don't need them), **Feelings** (remember others have them, too), **Forgive** (a most necessary attribute)

G - **Goals** (learn to set daily, weekly, life), **Giving** (always the best attitude), **Gold** (look for it in the sky, trees, fruit, flowers, grain, hills)

H - **Hope** (more than Pepsi, you gotta have it), **Help** (make a difference), **Happy** (an effort will do wonders), **Hugs** (to give and receive)

I - **Imitate** (the characteristics of three people you most admire), **Increase** (your worth by learning or working), **Initiate** (good works and ideas)

J - **Job** (is it time to try a new one?), **Join** (a support group or a class to learn something new)

K - **Knowledge** (never stop learning), **Kitchen** (should be the friendliest room in the house)

L - **Love** (greet each day with it), **Laugh** (it is the best medicine), **Live** (each day as though it is your last),

M - **Miracle** (you are nature's greatest, there is no other like you), **Meditate** (find your own special quiet place), **Music** (meant to be enjoyed)

N - **Now** (do everything you plan), **New** (treat yourself to something), **Notice** (everything in your world)

O - **Opportunity** (seize one), **Others** (offer a helping hand),

P - **Plan** (then do it), **Practice** (do it better), **Persist** (until you succeed), **Pray** (it is all right to ask for help), **Positive** (the best mental attitude)

Q - **Quiet** (everyone needs some), **Question** (a way to learn), **Quit** (bad habits - you know your own)

R - **Revive** (your spirit by your own personal method), **Renew** (your goals, your vows), **Receive** (the gift of life and love)

S - **Smile** (and the world smiles with you), **Self-Esteem** (build your own, by building others), **Survive** (you can), Sing (a happy song)

T - **Temptation** (avoid it), **Thanks** (take time to give it), **Teenagers** (if you must cope, ask for help)

U - **Understanding** (try to be, it may take effort)

V - **Victory** (you will achieve, if you master these ABCs)

W - **Wisdom** (takes a lot of practice), **Wonder** (never cease to marvel at all in the universe)

X - **Help X out all the bad**

Y - **Young** (practice a youthful attitude)

Z - **Zing** (now you've learned your ABCs)

Bibliography

BOOKS

Alexander, Shoshana. IN PRAISE OF SINGLE PARENTS. Boston: Houghton-Mifflin Company, 1994.6

Anderson, Joan. THE SINGLE MOTHER'S BOOK. Atlanta: Peachtree Publishers, 1990.

Bartlett, John. BARTLETT'S FAMILIAR QUOTATIONS. Boston: Little, Brown and Company, 1992.

The Bible, King James Version.

Bloomfield, Harold H., M.D., and Peter McWilliams. HOW TO HEAL DEPRESSION. Los Angeles, California: Prelude Press, 1994.

Branden, Nathaniel. HOW TO RAISE YOUR SELF-ESTEEM. New York: Bantam Books, 1987.

Bozarth-Campbell, Alla. LIFE IS GOODBYE, LIFE IS HELLO. Minneapolis: CompCare Publications, 1982.

Brothers, Dr. Joyce. WIDOWED. New York: Simon and Schuster, 1990.

———. POSITIVE PLUS, THE PRACTICAL PLAN FOR LIKING YOURSELF BETTER. NY: G. P. Putnam's Sons, 1982.

Chopra, Deepak. AGELESS BODY, TIMELESS MIND. New York: Harmony Books, 1993.

Cohen, Miriam Galper. LONG DISTANCE PARENTING. New York: New American Library, 1989.

Cousins, Norman. ANATOMY OF AN ILLNESS, New York: Norton, 1979.

DeFoore, Bill, Ph.D. ANGER, DEAL WITH IT, HEAL WITH IT, STOP IT FROM KILLING YOU. Deerfield Beach, Florida: Health Communications, Inc., 1991.

Falwell, Jerry. THE NEW AMERICAN FAMILY. Dallas, Texas: Word Publishing, 1992.

Friedman, Dr. Sonya with Guy Kettelhack. ON A CLEAR DAY YOU CAN SEE YOURSELF. Boston: Little , Brown and Company, 1991.

Gates, Philomene. SUDDENLY ALONE. New York: Harper & Row, Publishers, 1990.

Godfrey, Neal S. and Carolina Edwards. MONEY DOESN'T GROW ON TREES. New York: Simon & Schuster, 1994.

Helmstetter, Shad. YOU CAN EXCEL IN TIMES OF CHANGE. New York: Pocket Books, Simon and Schuster, Inc., 1991.

Hill, Napoleon and W. Clement Stone. SUCCESS THROUGH A POSITIVE MENTAL ATTITUDE. New York: Pocket Books, Simon and Schuster, 1977.

Hostetler, Dr. Jep. 10 THINGS PARENTS SHOULD KNOW ABOUT DRUG AND ALCOHOL ABUSE. Intercourse, PA.: Good Books, 1991.

Hudson, Pat. SOLUTION ORIENTED WOMAN. New York: W. W. Norton & Company, 1996.

Johnson, Otto, Ed. INFORMATION PLEASE ALMANAC 1997. New York: Houghton-Mifflin company, Inc., 1997.

Kornhaber, Arthur and Kenneth L. Woodward. GRAND-PARENTS, GRANDCHILDREN Garden City, N.Y.: Anchor Press/ Doubleday, 1981.

Leman, Dr. Kevin. KEEPING YOUR FAMILY TOGETHER WHEN THE WORLD IS FALLING APART. New York: Delacorte Press, 1992.

Lindsay, Rae. ALONE AND SURVIVING. New York: Walker and Company, 1977.

McCall, Edith. SOMETIMES WE DANCE ALONE. Brooklyn, New York: Brett Books, Inc., 1994.

McWilliams, Peter and John-Roger. DO IT! LET'S GET OFF OUR BUTS. Los Angeles: Prelude Press, 1991.

Mandino, Og. THE GREATEST GIFT IN THE WORLD. New York: Frederick Fell Pub. Inc., 1976.

Meyer, Roberta. LISTEN TO THE HEART. New York: Ballantine Books, 1988.

Myers, David G. THE PURSUIT OF HAPPINESS. New York: William Morrow & Company, Inc., 1992.

Stearns, Ann Kaiser. COMING BACK. New York: Ballantine Books, 1988.

Treadwell, Perry. MAKING FRIENDS, LEAVING LONELINESS BEHIND. Deerfield Beach, Florida: Health Communications, Inc., 1992).

MAGAZINES

Bartholomew, Anita. "Is Your Child Huffing?" *Reader's Digest* May 1996: 131-135.

Beathard, Ron. "My Turn - Over 40 and Un-Married." *Newsweek* 3 June 1996: 12.

Cavanaugh, Michael. "Pushing the Panic Button." *Christian Singles* July 1994: 17.

Chazin, Suzanne. "Teen Pregnancy, Let's Get Real." *Reader's Digest* Sept 1996: 49-52.

Davis, Susan. "The Enduring Power of Friendships." *American Health* July/August 1996: 59-62.

D'Aulaire, Per Ola and Emily. "How to Raise Drug-Free Kids." *Reader's Digest* April 1997: 150-160.

Dienstag, Eleanor Foa. "Living Alone." *New Choices,* 1997-1998

Dodson, Reynolds. "Our Angry Age" from Southhampton Press. *Reader's Digest* Aug 1995: 185.

Doskoch, Peter. "Happily Ever Laughter." *Psychology Today* July/August 1996: 33-35.

Fitzgerald, Randy. "You Can Make a Million." *Reader's Digest* July 1996: 25-32.

Gardner, John W. "Self-Renewal." *The Futurist* Nov/Dec 1996: 9-12.

Glassman, James K. "How to Build a Big Nest Egg." from Washington Post for *Reader's Digest* May, 1996: 45-48

Gordeeva, Ekaterina with E. M. Swift. "Finding My Way Back." *Reader's Digest* March 1997: 74-77.

Hannah, Dr. Jane. "Questions and Answers." *Christian Singles* July 1994: 24-25.

Keating, Peter. "Lotto Fever." from Money in *Reader's Digest* Oct 1996: 157-164.

Longo, Tracey. "How Singles Should Plan Their Finances." *Kiplinger's Personal Finance Magazine* May 1996: 81-83.

———. "Painless Ways To Tame Your Spending" *Kiplinger's Personal Finance Magazine* Jan 1996: 91-92.

Mason, Deborah. "Our World." *New Choices* Nov 1996:

McLanahan, Sara. "Double the Trouble." *Psychology Today* May/June 1996: 18.

Oshima, Sumiko. "Japan: Feeling the Strains of an Aging Population." *Science* 5 July 1996: 43-44.

Perry, Collin. "Help Yourself Through the Hard Times." *Reader's Digest* Feb 1997: 123-126.

Rennicke, Jeff. "How to find a Rainbow." condensed from Backpacker for *Reader's Digest* Sep 1996: 67-69.

Rouse, William B. "Discovering Who You Are and Where You are Headed." *The Futurist* Mar/Ap 1996: 38.

Scattarella, Christy. "My Opinion," *Parents* Sep 1996: 232.

Toufexis, Anastasia. "When the Ring doesn't fit..." *Psychology Today* Nov/Dec 1996: 52-55.